STRAIGHT UP
STOCK
INVESTING

STRAIGHT UP STOCK INVESTING

A COMPLETE FRAMEWORK FOR THE SERIOUS STOCK INVESTOR

ADAM DUNSBY

gatekeeper press

Tampa, Florida

Straight Up Stock Investing: A Complete Framework for the Serious Stock Investor

Published by Gatekeeper Press
7853 Gunn Hwy, Suite 209
Tampa, FL 33626
www.GatekeeperPress.com

Library of Congress Control Number: 2022946462

ISBN (paperback): 9781662932304
eISBN: 9781662932311

TABLE OF CONTENTS

PREFACE

What This Book Is About

This book provides a complete framework for investing in individual stocks. The framework consists of three pieces: identification, valuation, and personalization.

I show you why you need a framework. Why without one all that information in your head just bounces around and doesn't grow your wealth. Why without a framework you end up following the crowd and harboring nagging doubts about your investments. And why with a framework—the one I'll teach you—you'll become a confident and wealthier investor.

Identification is the first piece. Identification means finding the stocks you'd consider buying at the right price. Identification means finding your gold mine and staying in it. There are some qualities you want in the companies you invest in, and some qualities that you don't. I'll show you which is which. And I'll show you that *you* have unique abilities that give you a leg up, even if you don't know it.

Valuation is the second piece. Valuation means determining the intrinsic value of a share of a company. What it's really worth. I'll show you how to think about valuation and how to do it. And you don't need to worry about the math. Spreadsheets make it all a breeze.

Personalization is the third piece. Personalization means adopting the practices that lead to success and adjusting them to fit your circumstances. I'll teach you how to manage risk, how to size your positions, when to trade, and more. And I'll show you how to do these things in a way that fits your goals and situation.

And I'll also teach you the number 1 rule of investing. By knowing this one rule, you'll protect your wealth and always be ready for opportunity. Interested?

Who This Book Is For

This book is for serious investors who want to spend time on their investments, just not all their time. It's for investors who aren't satisfied with just being passive, who are willing to step forward and take control of their financial future. It's for investors who want their wealth to grow and want to know how to do it.

You want the steps.

Perhaps you've read books by great investors and received great advice but still struggle to create an action plan. Perhaps you've read books by brilliant hedge fund managers but still find what they do mysterious and out of reach. *Just tell me what to do*, you keep thinking.

This book tells you.

Readers should have some basic knowledge about stock markets—what a stock is, for instance. What a dividend is. This is not an introduction to the stock market. But if you have a retirement account or have ever bought a share of stock, you probably know enough to benefit from these pages.

To implement this approach, you need to be willing to devote some time. How much? When you're getting started—researching your companies, setting up your spreadsheets—you'll need to devote a few hours a week. After that, it's up to you. Like most pursuits, the more you put in, the more you'll get out. As Benjamin Franklin said, "The used key is always bright."

How This Book Is Structured

This book is divided into three sections, one for each of the pieces of the stock investing framework: identification, valuation, personalization.

Section 1 is identification. I start by explaining why it's important to have a list of stocks ready *before* you buy a single share. In the three chapters of this section, I explain how to build your list. I show you the company characteristics to be desired, the characteristics to be avoided, and how to tap into your unique skills and experiences to give you an advantage. (Yes, you have them!)

Section 2 is valuation. To know if a stock is cheap or expensive, you must first know what it's worth. I show you how to value companies. We start with the simplest model and work our way up. I show you why it's important to distinguish cash flows from earnings and why the internal rate of return is a great tool for evaluating investments.

Section 3 is personalization. Having constructed your list of potentials and valued them, you're almost there. Now you need to know how to pull it all together. How do you to stick to the plan? When do you trade? How much do you trade? When do you sell? How do you manage risk? I share my answers to these questions. But more important, I show you how to answer these questions for yourself, because your life, your goals, are unique to you.

The book concludes with the number 1 rule of investing. You don't want to learn this one the hard way.

INTRODUCTION

After receiving my PhD in finance, I entered the hedge fund industry. I worked on quantitative (algorithmic) models, managing hundreds of millions of dollars for investors. The models pulled in data, applied rules, and generated trades. I had much of my personal savings invested in these strategies, but not all.

The rest of my savings I managed myself. Like many investors, I turned to equities.

It didn't go well.

My self-image was that of a highly educated investment professional. Yet when it came to investing my personal savings in stocks, I jumped on tips and chased shiny objects. I took starter positions and bailed if things didn't go well. I always felt like I was in the dark about my own portfolio—even though I was the one who had bought the stocks. I wasn't fully confident in my holdings, and I certainly wasn't achieving the same success as with my professional investing.

But why?

I read the writings of the great investors. I talked to smart people. I even went to a few Berkshire Hathaway annual meetings. Why did it feel like I didn't know what I was doing?

My mission became to become a successful stock investor, and this book is the outcome of that quest.

First Steps

My first insight was to realize that where I was successfully investing—at work—I had a model. Computers inputted data, applied precise rules, and outputted positions.

My second insight was to realize that a model wouldn't work.

A fully quantitative model requires lots of computers, data feeds, software, and a full-time commitment. This wouldn't work for someone who wants to intelligently invest in equities but does something else for a living. Plus, the technology resources are out of reach for most.

But . . . I was heading in the right direction.

There was something else, too. I was always uncomfortable with one aspect of quantitative investing. It was a sophisticated approach, but it was also backward-looking. Quantitative models run on historical data: the price-earnings ratio, the recent change in price, and similar measures. There's no place for a view of the future. If Apple is about to introduce a new product or Pfizer is working on a promising new vaccine, there's no place for it in a model because it hasn't happened yet.

What I needed was a method to use the information I had in a structured way, while still having the flexibility to incorporate my outlook on the future. I needed a framework.

You Need a Framework for Investing in Stocks

I was well-informed. I knew the inflation rate, what Medtronic made, and who the CEO of JP Morgan was. But all that knowledge was just taking up space in my brain, undirected. Being well-informed and being effective, I learned, are not the same.

Just as adhering to a model is too rigid, just reacting to information is too scattered.

A framework is a way of organizing and using information to achieve an end. It's the steps one must take to reach a goal. In our case, it's the steps you must take to construct a portfolio of stocks that will increase in value.

A framework is not an algorithm. It's not just plugging numbers into a spreadsheet. It doesn't tell you not to think. A framework guides you toward the information you need and tells you what to do with the information you have. A framework is a hybrid of a model and your wisdom.

Without a framework, you just listen to what other people tell you about investing. You follow the crowd. If you read an article on value stocks, you buy value stocks. If you read an article on tech stocks, you switch to tech stocks. Before you know it, you're back to value stocks.

With a framework, you use your knowledge in a structured way to make good investment decisions. With a framework, you have the confidence that comes from understanding what you're doing. When the market drops, you won't panic. Your friends come to you for advice. You become one of the smart people.

The Straight Up Stock Investing Framework

Over the years, I developed a framework for stock investing that 1) uses information in a disciplined way and 2) is forward looking. This book presents this framework.

I've had great successes, such as buying Microsoft at prices in the twenties and Apple in the teens (much of which I still hold as I write this). Of course, I've had failures too, such as owning Washington Mutual (a former savings bank) going into the 2008 financial crisis.

But even in the face of my mistakes I found myself a sturdier investor. After 2008, when investors were fleeing financial stocks, I was able to assess the situation from an approach I had confidence in. Sure, I suffered losses like everyone else, but I didn't panic sell. I held onto banks such as JP Morgan, which rose from the ashes and reached new heights.

The Straight Up Stock Investing framework has three parts: Identification, Valuation, and Personalization.

Identification

Identification means finding the stocks that you'd consider buying at the right price.

Counterintuitively, this requires you to *narrow* the universe of stocks you follow. But isn't it better to follow more stocks to have more options? This would be true if you were a cyborg and could comprehend thousands of stocks, but you're not. There are thousands of companies out there, and there's just no way to know a meaningful amount about all of them.

Can't I just learn about a stock after someone really smart tells me it's a good buy? Smart people are a good source of investment leads. So if someone you respect recommends you buy XYZ, researching XYZ and possibly adding it to your list of potentials makes sense. But if you're just investing a few minutes learning about a company before going out and buying it, you're making a mistake. Furthermore, after doing this a few times, you'll stop even investing the few minutes of research and just give yourself over to the opinions of others.

Identification also requires you to focus on good companies. Companies in good industries with good growth prospects. Growth is the great tailwind of investing. Conversely, you want to avoid companies in shrinking and unprofitable industries. It's almost never worth buying shares in a company whose profits are declining.

Identification is where you bring in your skills, experiences, and passions. You may not be a professional investor, but if you work in the software industry you know more about software than the average Wall

Street analyst. If each year you can't wait to learn every car company's upcoming lineup, that passion will give insights into the auto industry.

What if you don't have experiences relevant to a particular industry? No problem! If you're energized to succeed, you're more than halfway there. Many of today's great investors started as generalists. You'll just have to invest the time researching companies and industries you think are promising. But it won't feel like work, it will be an exciting exploration!

Your list of potential investments is your gold mine.

Valuation

Valuation means figuring out what a share of a company's stock is worth—its intrinsic value.

Companies can be exciting, and they can be boring. Companies can make products that make you happy, like ice cream, and they can make products that make you yawn, like insurance. But none of this determines the intrinsic value of a company.

As a shareholder, what you get is your share of the earnings a firm generates in the future. To value a company, you must add up all those future earnings the right way. The good news for today's investors is that with spreadsheets, those calculations are easy. This book will show you the exact steps you need to compute a company's real value.

Personalization

Personalization means adopting the habits and practices that lead to success and adjusting them to fit your circumstances.

We'll learn how to manage risk, how to size positions, how often to trade, and more. Many of the lessons will be counterintuitive. For instance, I'll tell you why you should never take small positions and why you shouldn't make a trade whenever a good opportunity comes along. And I'll also tell you the number 1 rule of investing.

A Final Thought

The Straight Up Stock Investing approach isn't just a value approach, and it isn't just a growth approach. Both approaches have merit, so why limit ourselves? Why not consider the price today as well as the earnings on the horizon? Why not invest in companies we think are great, at prices we think are great, with an approach we believe in?

Let's get started.

Part I:
IDENTIFICATION

Chapter 1:
QUALITIES OF GOOD STOCKS

Before we get into the question of *how* to value a stock, we'll first deal with the question of *what* to value. There are around three thousand stocks listed on the New York Stock Exchange, and there's no way you can follow them all. What we need to do is narrow the universe of stocks we follow. That way, when we go looking for good investments, we'll have a pool from which we can start our search. A collection of stocks that we've thought about, collected data on, and believe are businesses with good long-term prospects.

What about just learning about a stock on the fly? You read an article that makes a compelling case for Flying Widget Industries. Why not just figure it all out right then?

If you needed heart surgery, would you call up your cousin who's a high school guidance counselor and ask him to study bypass surgery so he could operate on you next week? Okay, maybe that's a bit dramatic. Let's try this. Say you needed someone to give a twenty-minute lecture on Abraham Lincoln. Most Americans have learned something about Lincoln in school. Most of us could review the Wikipedia article and get up and talk about Lincoln for a few minutes. But wouldn't someone who's studied Lincoln in an organized way over an extended time give a better talk? Someone who's established a foundation of knowledge? Of course they would.

It's hard to interpret information at the same time you're establishing a foundation on which to interpret that information.

The second reason you should have a prepared list of potentials is that it naturally leads to comparison with other potential investments. You might read a great case for Flying Widget, but how do you know some other stock isn't a better investment? If you have a list of stocks you're following, you'll compare an investment in Flying Widget to your other options and maybe find a better one.

But the third and most important reason is that making investment decisions in the moment—whether based on an article, a tip from a friend, or a wave of group excitement—will cause you to backslide into crowd following. Having engaged in adrenaline investing, it won't take much to cede your independence and just do what everyone else is doing.

Considering only companies with good long-term prospects is key. We'll want to limit ourselves to businesses that have a promising future. Of course, what we're really interested in are companies that have strong and growing cash flows. But starting with three thousand financial statements isn't practical. It's easier to approach it from the other direction. We'll start with the qualities that are likely to lead to the earning power and then find companies that have these qualities.

Conversely, we'll want to avoid companies that have poor long-term prospects. Whatever the price, it's hard to make money in a stock if the industry or the company has a dim outlook. But no need to worry. There are plenty of great companies out there. So many that you won't be able to track them all.

Now, you might ask: Can't so-so companies sometimes get undervalued, and can't you make money buying them when they do? The answer is yes, but it's not ideal. Say a company, SosoCo, doesn't have earnings growth and has a long-term price-to-earnings ratio of 10. It trades down to a P/E[1] of 8, and you buy it. You've made a good trade, and SosoCo trades back up to a P/E of 10—its price has gone up. But now what do you do? The stock is now fairly valued, so you sell it. You pay the capital

---

1	The P/E ratio is the stock price divided by earnings. We'll talk more about it in chapter 4.

gains taxes, you pay some transaction costs, and now you must find something else to invest your money in. Not bad, but better to invest in a company that will grow its earnings over time. If you've gotten in at a reasonable price, those rising earnings will cause the stock price and the dividends to rise over time.

I personally track a list of about fifty stocks. It's grown over the years, and I adjust from time to time, adding or deleting companies whose prospects have changed. I recommend starting with ten to twenty companies and lengthening your list as time goes on.

In this chapter, we're going to talk about the qualities we'd like to see in the companies we'd consider investing in. In the following chapter, we'll get into what companies to avoid. And in the chapter after that, we'll talk about something really interesting: You.

Industry Has Great Long-Term Prospects

Before we talk about individual companies, let's talk about the industry that a company belongs to. It's hard to make money in the long term in an industry that is in decline. A good company in a bad industry can outperform for a while, but eventually the weight of decline will bring it down too. When the horse and buggy industry went south, it took all the horse and buggy makers with it, no matter how well they executed.

Unfortunately, the converse is not true. Bad companies in good industries don't do well. Some companies just execute poorly or are too late to the market. Energy and financial markets are two of the best industries to have been in over the past century. But through bad management and corrupt leaders, Enron, a onetime powerhouse in both, collapsed.

There are many, many industries that will do well over time. We live in a time of great economic prosperity. Just by paying attention to what's going on in the world you're aware of lots of them. Software, medicine, home building, finance—these are just some of the industries that we'll always need and will grow in the future.

And there are also industries that will have a tougher go of it. Print media has been decimated by the internet, and there's no turnaround in sight for them. Online shopping knocked storefront retail down a peg. It will be interesting to see what happens to the fossil fuel industry. Here the trends are being driven not by economics but by societal pressure to replace carbon-emitting energy with renewable energy.

How do you identify the promising industries? Start by asking yourself this: Do you see this industry growing or shrinking in the future? Will people want more of its product or less? Will it displace an existing technology or be displaced? How about video games? Check, check, check. The industry is growing; people love the product; it is displacing other recreational activities.

Another approach is to identify the earnings trend of the biggest companies in the industry. A whole industry can't luck into strong earnings growth. If earnings are steadily increasing, there's probably something good going on.

The basic point is this: Some industries have the wind at their back. Some industries have the wind in their face. You'll do better with the wind at your back.

Earnings Growth

"Over the long term, it's hard for a stock to earn a much better return than the business which underlies it earns." This is from Charlie Munger's 1994 address, "A Lesson on Elementary, Worldly Wisdom as It Relates to Investment Management & Business." This is the best article written on stock investing, and this quote captures a core principle.

The longer you hold a stock, the more your return will be a function of the company's earnings growth and the less it will be of the stock's initial valuation. To put together a collection of companies you'd consider owning for the long term, you should focus on companies with strong or at least decent earnings growth.

I'll illustrate this by example, but before that let's define one term. A company's price-earnings ratio is its current stock price divided by its earnings. Usually, *earnings* is taken to mean the most recent twelve months' earnings, but sometimes it is a forward-looking estimate. The price-earnings ratio is the most common measure of a stock's valuation. The lower the price-earnings ratio, the cheaper the stock. For the purposes of the following example, let's assume the long-term price-earnings ratio of all stocks is 15.

Consider the following Figure 1.1:

Figure 1.1.

Company	growth/ yr	P/E	Earnings	Price	P/E	Earnings	Price	IRR
			Year 0			**Year 5**		
A	10%	20	$10.00	$200.00	15	$16.11	$241.58	3.85%
B	0%	10	$10.00	$100.00	15	$10.00	$150.00	8.45%

Say we have two companies, A and B. Company A trades at a P/E of 20 and B trades at a P/E of 10. So, as measured by P/E, B is cheaper. A P/E of 10 versus 20. For simplicity, we'll assume they both have earnings today of $10 per share. If we multiply the price-earnings ratio by earnings, earnings cancel out, and we get the price.

Company A: 20 * 10 = $200/share.

Company B: 10 * 10 = $100/share.

But now let's assume that company A grows earnings by 10 percent a year, while B has no earnings growth. Company B's earnings stay fixed at $10. Company A has a high P/E, suggesting overvaluation, but it also has high earnings growth. Company B, on the other hand, has a low P/E, suggesting undervaluation, but it has low earnings growth. (For simplicity, we'll assume earnings get reinvested into the operations of the companies.)

Let's say we buy A and B and hold them for five years. In five years, the P/E ratios for both A and B go to 15, the long-term equilibrium. Company A's earnings grow 10 percent a year to $16.11/share, and B's stay where they are at $10/share. So the share price for company A in five years is $241.58, and the share price for B is $150/share, just B's earnings of $10/share times it's new P/E of 15.

Which produces a higher return after five years? Company B. With B, you earn 8.45 percent a year, while Company A earns 3.85 percent a year. In this case, B's undervaluation wins out over A's higher growth.

But what if we hold for ten years, keeping everything else the same? Refer to Figure 1.2.

Figure 1.2.

		Year 0			Year 10			
Company	growth/ yr	P/E	Earnings	Price	P/E	Earnings	Price	IRR
A	10%	20	$10.00	$200.00	15	$25.94	$389.06	6.88%
B	0%	10	$10.00	$100.00	15	$10.00	$150.00	4.14%

Now company A pulls ahead, 6.88 percent for A compared to 4.14 percent for B. This time, higher earnings growth wins. As it turns out, the longer the holding period, the better Company A, the growth company, does compared to Company B.

To bring this into higher relief, let's consider a fifty-year holding period, as shown in Figure 1.3.

Figure 1.3.

Company	growth/yr	P/E	Earnings	Price	P/E	Earnings	Price	IRR
			Year 0			Year 50		
A	10%	20	$10.00	$200.00	15	$1173.91	$17608.63	9.37%
B	0%	10	$10.00	$100.00	15	$10.00	$150.00	0.81%

Now the difference is even more pronounced. The annual return is 9.37 percent for Company A, and 0.81 percent for Company B. The longer you hold, the closer Company A gets to a return of 10 percent, its growth rate, and the closer B gets to a return of zero, its growth rate. Over the long term, growth is everything and undervaluation is nothing.

This is why dismissing high P/E stocks is a mistake. A high P/E may be justified if the company has high earnings growth. When Warren Buffett bought Coca-Cola in 1988, the P/E was around 15. Not a nosebleed P/E, but one that hardcore value investors would have skipped. More recently, Amazon has traded at high P/E's but has also produced earnings growth well into the double digits. You need to consider both today's price and *future* earnings to make an informed decision.

The lesson here is: Companies on your list of potentials should have at least some growth in earnings.

Valuable Intangible

An intangible is something that does not have form but does have value.

The most prominent example is a brand name. People are often willing to go with a brand they are familiar with. They trust it and may have developed a positive emotional association with it. Say you've drunk Coca-Cola your whole life. If you're in the grocery store and there's Coke and a generic brand for a few cents less, what are you going to do? You're going to pick up the Coke. And those few cents add up. In 2020, Forbes estimated the value of the Coca-Cola brand to be $64 billion.[2] And Coke isn't even close to the most valuable brand. Forbes estimated Apple's brand to be worth $241 billion.

There are other valuable intangibles. Consider patents, which grant creators the exclusive rights to their inventions for several years. This is particularly important to the pharmaceutical industry, in which companies spend to develop new drugs and then have exclusive right to them for a period. They also are very important in the technology industry.

Another valuable intangible is a copyright. Consider these characters: Mickey Mouse, Spider-Man, and Bugs Bunny. These characters are protected by copyrights. That companies are always lobbying Congress to extend copyright protection suggests that these copyrights are valuable. I would guess the copyright on Spider-Man alone is worth billions.

Now, not all intangible assets are worth something. The firm must be able to monetize it, such as by making a Spider-Man movie. I would bet that most patents have produced no value to their creators, but some have produced a lot.

---

2   Marty Swant, "The World's Most Valuable Brands," Forbes.com, https://www. forbes.com/the-worlds-most-valuable-brands/#46200d7f119c (accessed September 28, 2022).

~~Good~~ Great Management

It's hard to measure, but there's no getting around that management matters. Try to imagine Apple without Steve Jobs, Amazon without Jeff Bezos, or Walt Disney without, well, Walt Disney. I doubt Tesla would even exist without Elon Musk, let alone achieved the heights it has reached.

Of course, these managers are also founders and visionaries. But that isn't necessary. What matters is that management is honest, focused, and has a history of making good decisions. Jamie Dimon did not found JP Morgan, but he's focused and more often than not makes good decisions. Steve Jobs didn't have a reputation for being a nice guy, but he did have a reputation for being incredibly focused on creating great products. (A good book about managers that have shone for their investors is *The Outsiders* by William N. Thorndike Jr.)

A CEO who has made good decision after good decision likely has a lot of good decisions in their future. A company led by a CEO who has made a lot of bad decisions is one you want to leave off your list. Common bad decisions are expensive acquisitions outside a company's core business, mismanaging crises, and standing flat-footed while competitors adopt new technology. If a CEO spends all their time advocating for social causes that may be great for society, you should wonder who is minding the shop.

Nothing takes out a company faster than corrupt management. Remember WorldCom? No? At the turn of the century, it was one of the biggest communication companies in the United States. But an accounting scandal pushed it into bankruptcy and sent CEO Bernie Ebbers to prison. If you don't trust a company's management, stay away.

Monopoly or Oligopoly

When an industry is controlled by one or a small number of companies, those companies will often do well. It's pretty simple: If you don't have much competition, you can charge more. In some cases, you can charge whatever you want.

For years, Microsoft had an effective monopoly on computer operating systems. If you wanted a useful PC, you had to use MS-DOS, then MS Windows. Users were often frustrated by the quality of the operating system, but it didn't matter—they were the only show in town.

Monopolies don't have to span the globe or the country; they can be regional. For instance, railroad companies are often the only railroads in the region in which they operate. They may face competition from trucks, but not other railroads.

Another example is your local electric company. I bet you only have one, and you must receive your electricity from them. In some cases, the government recognizes a monopoly naturally exists (that is, it's not efficient to have more than one company offering the service), and they regulate the returns the company can earn.

Related to monopoly is when a company controls a pinch point in the value chain. For example, Home Depot and Lowe's are big buyers of hardware. If you're a producer of hardware equipment, you're going to want to sell to Home Depot and Lowe's. Since Home Depot and Lowe's have lots of producers to buy from, they can dictate terms. On the retail side, Home Depot and Lowe's are the easiest places for consumers to shop—they have the widest selections. So they can charge higher prices to consumers. Paying less for the product you buy, then charging more when you sell to consumers is a good gig. This is what you can do when you control a pinch point in the value chain.

For the companies on your potential list, market power is a big plus.

Network Effect

The idea of the network effect is that some products produce more value to each user the more users there are. Consider a social network. If you want to be on the social media site that all your friends are on, and your friends want to be on the site that all their friends are on, then soon everyone is on the same social media site. And that site can make a lot of money selling advertising. This, of course, is Facebook.

If you want to shop in online auctions, you want to go where the most sellers are. And if you want to sell, you want to be where the most shoppers are. Eventually, you just have one auction site. This dynamic drove eBay to prominence.

An example that is so woven into our lives that it's easy to overlook is the cell phone. The cell phone is only useful because the people you want to talk to have them. If the people you wanted to talk to used walkie-talkies or Zoom or smoke signals, a phone would be much less useful. And the phone companies would make much less money.

The network effect doesn't have to operate through the internet, but the internet has increased its importance. The internet allows unlimited numbers of people to come together.

As an aside, the network effect is why breaking up Facebook into two social media companies doesn't make sense. If the government broke Facebook up into Facebook 1 and Facebook 2, eventually users would all gravitate to one and the other would go out of business. We'd be back where we started.

Companies that have established themselves as the hub of a network are worthy of consideration.

High Switching Costs

I've used the same accountant for my taxes for over twenty-five years. Now, I love my accountant, but even if I didn't, would I switch? Don't tell Mark this, but probably not. If I switched to a new accountant, I'd have to root around for all sorts of past returns and documents that Mark already has. It would be a pain in the neck. In this context, the technical term for pain in the neck is *switching cost.*

Like Mark, businesses can benefit from high switching costs. Say, for instance, a company buys a software package to maintain its customer database and trains all its employees on the software. If a new software package comes along that's a little bit better or a little bit cheaper, will it switch? Not for a little bit. The company would have to retrain its whole workforce. The switching cost is high, so it stays with its current vendor.

Or say your mechanics are all trained to maintain John Deere equipment, and a Caterpillar salesman comes along and offers you a deal. Will you switch? It would have to be a great deal because you're going to incur a big expense in money and time to retrain all your mechanics.

While it's great to benefit from high switching costs, if that's all a company has going for it, it probably won't be enough. If a competitor keeps offering a better deal or a superior product, eventually customers will switch. And then the competitor will become the beneficiary of high switching costs. If a company is failing in other ways, high switching costs can only protect it for so long.

Low-Cost Producer

Sometimes a company can just produce a product or service cheaper than everyone else. This allows them to offer it for a lower price while still making a good profit.

Scale is one way to do this. Once Walmart achieved such huge economies of scale, it was hard for any physical store to compete with them. The grocery chains that napped while Walmart relentlessly invested and grew one day found themselves with a choice to make. They could also make immense investment in stores and supply chain, or they could hope for the best. Hope turned out to be a bad strategy. The people who wanted the lowest prices went to Walmart.

A low-cost producer can also be one that has a cheap source of a resource. Saudi Arabia can drill oil cheaper than anyone else on the planet. They can be profitable at prices low enough to drive most private companies out of business.

Dividends

Dividends shouldn't affect the value of a firm. After all, as a shareholder, you own the company. If a company keeps a dollar in the bank or gives it to you, it's still your dollar. It's no different than taking a dollar out of your left pocket and putting it into your right pocket. Later in this book, when we construct our valuation model, dividends won't even appear.

But . . . dividends can tell you about a firm's management. If a company needs to invest everything it has to grow its core business, that's one thing. But if a company has tons of cash and is just sitting on it, you must wonder. Are the leaders looking to use that money to entertain themselves through an unrelated merger? Can they justify higher compensation with a bigger market cap? Are they most interested in having an empire? CEOs that retain cash they don't need may not be shareholder-oriented.

Share repurchases can also be an indicator of shareholder-oriented management. But paying a dividend is a stronger indicator. Firms hate to cut dividends. At a minimum, it's embarrassing to the CEO. So once a firm starts paying a dividend, it is implicitly committing to keep paying it.

A side note on share repurchases: price matters. If a company's stock is overvalued and it repurchases shares, it's making things worse for its remaining shareholders. If the intrinsic value of a company's shares is $60 and it buys them back at $100, it's destroying $40 every time it buys back a share. The home builders that undertook big repurchase programs right before the 2008 crash vaporized a lot of shareholder money.

The bottom line on dividends is that they provide evidence that the firm is shareholder-oriented.

Am I Just Too Late?

In his book *Zero to One*, Peter Thiel states his go-to interview question: "What important truth do very few people agree with you on?"

Here's my answer: You can be late to an industry trend and still make money.

Back in high school in the eighties, I stocked shelves at Laneco on Route 22 in New Jersey. Mr. J, the assistant manager (we didn't call him Mr. J, I just can't remember the rest of his name), told me that computers seemed like a good thing and he was going to encourage his kids to go into that business.

Computers? Over low-end retail? This was the eighties! Microsoft was founded in 1975, Apple in 1976. Sorry, Mr. J (or whatever), you're ten years too late!

As it turned out—no.

Over the ensuing decades you would have had many opportunities to invest in Microsoft, Apple, and numerous other computer and software companies and make fantastic returns.

An industry that's been a great industry for a long time will probably continue to be a great industry for a long time. So don't worry if everyone knows one of your potentials is a great company in a great industry. Put it on your list anyway. You may just get the chance to buy it at a good price.

Summary

Make a list of the companies you'd consider investing in at the right price. This is your gold mine that you'll return to over and over. Why even look in the guano mine? The characteristics you want to see in your gold mine stocks are these: great long-term prospects for the industry, strong earnings growth, a valuable intangible, great management, monopoly or oligopoly, network effect, high switching costs, low-cost producer, and pays dividends. There are others too, but you won't go wrong limiting your stock investments to companies that possess the characteristics on this list. Remember, you're not buying every stock on this list, but you're going to be ready when one of these stocks gets cheap.

That's the good. But there's also the bad. We'll turn to the characteristics you'd rather not see in a company next.

Chapter 2:
QUALITIES OF BAD STOCKS

Just as there are qualities you'd like to see in companies you'd consider investing in, there are qualities you'd like to avoid. In this chapter, we'll address those less desirable characteristics that make it hard for companies to make outsize returns. Of course, you can always just restate the good qualities as negatives. (The opposite of good management is bad management.) But in this chapter, we'll focus on a few characteristics that benefit from their own discussion. You'll want to leave any companies that possess these bad characteristics off your list of potentials.

Commodity Business

How many landscapers are on the Forbes 400? None. Why? Isn't landscaping important? It sure is, but it's hard for any individual landscaper to stand out in a way that customers are willing to pay up for. They're in a commodity business.

Commodity businesses are those where you can't differentiate your product. Typically, anyone can do it, and lots of people do. Sometimes the phrase *commodity business* is limited to physical commodities—like wheat or charging cords—but I use it more broadly to include services that are plain vanilla. Other examples of commodity businesses are growing corn, running a laundromat, making nails, changing oil, and you can probably think of plenty of others.

Consider for a moment solar panels. Everyone agrees that solar energy will be a big part of our energy future. But as far as I know, no one earns outsize profits making them. Why? Because they're not that hard to make, and customers don't care whose solar panels they use. I have solar panels on my house, and I have no idea who made them. There's a lesson here: Just because something is categorized as technology or is expected to be the wave of the future does not mean it will produce big profits.

Producers of commodity products and services have no pricing power. If there is demand for the product, then the producer should earn some return over time—but that's it. If they raise their price, customers will just go to someone else.

A partial exception to this rule is when a commodity is in short supply. It's still the case that one producer can't charge more than another, but demand will drive up the price for everyone, resulting in high profits until more supply can be produced. Think oil and OPEC. Over much of the twentieth century, oil demand pushed the limits of supply and oil-producing companies and countries made a lot of money.

Lots of Competition

If you're trying to make money, competition is bad. In a competitive industry, if you raise your price all your customers will go find someone cheaper. In a competitive industry, consumers extract almost all the value produced.

Consider airlines. They are famously unprofitable. Their bankruptcy attorneys make more than their shareholders. Why? Part of the reason is competition. You might pay a little more to fly, say, United, but not a lot. And if one airline comes up with an innovation that passengers like, all the other airlines will copy it. The industry would probably be better off if no one had a frequent flyer program. But if one does it, the others have to follow.

Or consider the auto industry: GM, Ford, Stellantis (Chrysler), Tesla, Volkswagen, Toyota, Honda, BMW, and so on. And that's before we even get to electric vehicle start-ups. That's a lot of companies trying to sell you a car. Sure, they compete on several dimensions such as features and reputation, but they also compete on price. Charge too much and customers look somewhere else. On top of this, some countries believe that having a local auto industry is of national importance and prop up their home auto companies even when a competitive market would have it otherwise.

Strong Unions

Industrial unions may be good for society, but for companies' profitability, not so much. Firms, of course, know this, which is why they always oppose unionization campaigns. When things are going well for a company, unions always step up and demand a greater share. Because they can organize strikes or slowdowns, companies often just give in. Unions also demand and usually get rigid job descriptions. This makes it tough for companies to adopt new technologies and be flexible, since workers would have to do things not in their current job description. Firms that are facing unionization may preemptively raise compensation.

Require a Lot of Capital Expenditure

Some businesses by their nature require large, ongoing capital expenditures. For instance, railroads must continually invest in tracks and railroad cars. Tracks wear out from weather and use. Trains only last so long.

Mining companies must always buy new equipment. Cruise lines have to buy new ships and maintain the ones they have. In general, industrial businesses require a lot of investment in plant and equipment. This is money that must be spent simply to maintain the existing business.

Capital-intensive companies must earn that much more before they have money to expand or to give back to shareholders.

Contrast this to an internet company such as Google. These companies have very little capital expenditure (capex). They're what we call capital-lite businesses. They have to buy some servers, and after that it's mostly just office supplies. Since they don't need to keep buying huge amounts of capital equipment, they generate lots of free cash flow.

High capital expenditures can also make a company's reported earnings harder to interpret. We'll get into this in detail later in the book. For now, companies must replace worn-out capital goods at current (higher) prices. But for income statement purposes, they must expense previous purchases at past (lower) prices. This makes reported earnings greater than the cash the company is generating (because the reported expense is less than the actual cash being spent).

Now, most companies need to make capital expenditures, so it's not something you need to run from. But you should be aware of the issues it presents.

A different problem capital expenditure can present is when technology changes and a company must spend a lot of money on new equipment just to keep up. This is illustrated in what I'll call the "Parable of the Mill" from the Charlie Munger article. The early Berkshire Hathaway, before it became what it is today, was a textile business. One day someone presented Warren Buffett a new loom that would do twice as much work as the existing looms. Warren Buffett said, "I hope this doesn't work because if it does, I'm going to close the mill." What was the problem? Textiles were a competitive business. As the textile mills switched to the new looms, the price of textiles would drop. All the benefit of the new technology would go to the consumer while all the cost of buying the looms would be borne by the mills.

This presents an important lesson. New technology isn't always good for companies' bottom lines. Sometimes all the benefit goes to the consumer. An interesting contemporary example is 5G in telecommunications. Everyone agrees that 5G is going to allow society to have significantly improved communications and make the internet of things more real. But ATT, Verizon, and T-Mobile are having to spend billions to upgrade their equipment and to buy the wavelengths from the government. If they don't do this, they will be left behind. So 5G is great for consumers, but is it good for the companies? To me, it's not clear. I own telecommunications companies, but I do wonder.

If a company has market power, cost savings are great and go to profit. If a pharmaceutical company has a patent on a drug and figures out how to make it cheaper, the savings will go to its bottom line. But if a company doesn't have pricing power, the savings go to the consumer, even if the company had to pay to achieve those savings.

Summary

That's the list of bad characteristics: commodity business, lots of competition, strong unions, lots of capex needed to keep up—all high hurdles to profitability. Any single one is not a deal breaker (all firms have some capex), but they make it tougher.

Note that both the auto and the airline industry suffer from strong competition, large capital requirements, and strong unions. This explains why these industries struggle to produce good returns for their shareholders.

Chapter 3:
YOU!

In the 1950s, Ernie Trefz was a manager at a meat packing company in Bridgeport, Connecticut.[3] He couldn't help but notice that a lot of meat was being delivered to this new restaurant chain, something called McDonald's. Ernie and his brother Chris decided they could do better than meat packing and started opening McDonald's restaurants themselves. Today, their family owns dozens of McDonald's franchises in Connecticut. They have produced great wealth for themselves and have generously supported the community.

Working at McKinsey in the late 1960s, John Malone developed an understanding of the cable television industry. He liked its predictable revenue, he liked its favorable tax treatment, and he liked its explosive growth. He liked its prospects so much he decided cable television would be his career. Good call. Malone ended up running cable giant TCI for decades, and today he is one of the richest people and largest landowners in America.[4]

Does company X belong to an industry that's going to boom in the future or to one that's going to stagnate? It could depend on many things, such as consumer preferences, how technology evolves, or the decision of a court. Is the CEO of company X a visionary or stuck in the past? Is a major competitor about to enter or exit the market? These important questions have one thing in common: the answer isn't a number that can be read off a screen and entered into a spreadsheet.

But *you* might know the answers.

---

3   Conversation with family members; see "History," Trefzmcdonalds.com (accessed September 28, 2022).

4   See William N. Thorndike Jr, *The Outsiders* (Boston: Harvard Business Review Press, 2012), 83–108.

If you run a restaurant, you'll have insight into trends in dining and what payment software is gaining popularity. If you're a doctor, maybe you know about medical devices or the pharmaceutical industry. If you work at a car dealership, you see the auto industry from the inside. You can build on this knowledge.

Your professional experiences can give you a leg up in putting together your list of potentials. If your professional experience leads you to think the architectural software industry is going to boom, you can research companies with exposure to that industry. Even better, maybe your professional experience provides insight into *which* architectural software companies have a competitive advantage.

If you've concluded an industry is going to lag, that's helpful too. Now you know to stay away from it. You've just narrowed your list of companies!

What about your education? This can be a big help too. Got a degree in computer engineering? Most people will never understand computer hardware at the level you did the day you got your diploma. Let that skill help you in evaluating computer companies.

What are your passions? Video games? Fashion? Sports? Those are all huge industries. You can use the knowledge you've gained having fun as a stepping-off point to understand those pursuits from a business perspective. Where is the fashion industry going? Rap replacing heavy metal? Maybe you should avoid those guitar stocks.

What if your professional or educational experiences aren't much help? That's okay. Many of the world's greatest investors have been generalists who entered the investment industry right out of school. You'll just need to put in the work researching companies and industries. I bet you have some interests. You can start there. Even if you don't find prospects in an industry that entices you, you'll gain experience that you can apply to the next industry you decided to research.

Tap into your network of friends. What businesses do they think have good prospects? Where have they made meaningful investments? If they've worked out, believe me, they'll love to tell you about it. But don't take their word for it. Use what they tell you as a lead to start your own investigation. Ask them who they talked to, what they read, what would make them change their minds. Ask them why, why, why? If you don't ask, you don't get.

Read, read, read! I start my day reading the *Wall Street Journal* pretty much cover to cover. Prefer the *Times* or *The Washington Post*? Great! Read that. Reading builds your knowledge base and keeps you exposed to trends. Read books on industry, businesses, and science. I find books written by founders are full of insights. But read all the time. It's one of the best things you can do to improve your long-term investing performance.

As a reminder, at this stage, don't worry about the price of a stock (we'll get to that). For now, you're just trying to construct a list of companies with good long-term prospects. And the point here is that you probably have more useful experience than you might think. How you achieved your experience and what form it takes is unique to you.

Now, you may think there's more to life than money, and you may want to combine your investing with other societal goals. This could mean you won't invest in tobacco companies, or that you want to invest in companies in your community. Or it could mean that you are full on board with ESG investing (environmental, social, and governance). ESG investing means placing significant weight on societal outcomes when choosing which companies to invest in.

If you go down this path, your societal goals will guide you to add companies to your list that wouldn't otherwise qualify on economic grounds and to keep off companies that otherwise would qualify on economic considerations. This is up to you. You don't want to own stocks that make you feel guilty. But do keep in mind that restricting your list for non-economic reasons can only lower your returns.

You have some valuable knowledge. Use it.

Summary

Whether you know it or not, you have knowledge unique to you that will help you find great companies to invest in: your job, your education, your passions, your friends. Use it!

PART II: VALUATION

Chapter 4:
THE BASIC MODEL

We've researched and assembled a group of companies we'd be excited to own at the right price. In this chapter, we're going to figure out what that right price is. We are going to need some math, but two things on that: First, we'll construct our model in steps, so it will be easy to follow. Second, you won't actually need to do any calculations or remember any formulas. Spreadsheets, such as Excel, can do all of that for you.

The basic idea is to figure out what we'd pay for all the firm's future earnings today. To give that number a name, let's call it intrinsic value. Then we compare the intrinsic value to the current stock price. If the current price is above the value of the future earnings, we avoid it or consider selling if we own it. If the price is well below the intrinsic value, we'll consider buying it. How far below? I look for stocks that trade at 60 percent or less of fair value.

Now you might be asking: If we're going to be valuing future earnings anyway, why did we need to make a list of good companies? The answer is this: When you categorize a company as good, you're saying something about its future earnings. You're confident the earnings stream is safe, that it will grow over time, and that earnings growth will lead to a higher real worth today. Also, there are too many companies to value them all.

Value the Whole Company

Remember that lemonade stand you had as a kid? All that mattered was how much you spent on lemonade mix and how much the people who pulled over paid you. Whether you put the money in your pocket or left it in the cup didn't make any difference. It was still your money. If your kid brother got bored, you gave him his share and he wandered off. The lemonade stand made just as much money as before; you just no longer had a partner, and all the future profits were yours. The lemonade stand was worth the profits it generated, and the value of your ownership was the share of the profits you got. This lemonade stand model also works for valuing stocks.

To value a share of stock we will 1) value the whole business, and 2) allocate the value based on the proportion of ownership that share represents. That is, we'll take the stance that the shareholders own all the future earnings. The biggest most complex corporation will be valued using the same method we would use to value a lemonade stand. This is sometimes called the value of a company to a private owner and is often attributed to Ben Graham.[5]

This approach seems obvious, but it contains some subtle points. First, a company *can* be valued. Not everyone has always thought that. For instance, adherents to a strong version of market efficiency take the view that whatever the share price is, that's the right price. By trading over time, the large number of market participants impart their information, leading to a price that incorporates all this information and is therefore the right price.

Now the Efficient Markets Theory is an easy thing to beat up on, and we're not going to do it here—it has far fewer proponents than it used to. When I was getting my PhD in finance in the 1990s, lots of finance professors were starting investment companies with strategies designed to beat the market. So academics as a group have had an elastic view of market efficiency for a long time.

Of course, this doesn't mean it's easy to make money trading financial instruments. If markets were wildly inefficient, we'd all be billionaires.

---

5   See Benjamin Graham, *The Intelligent Investor*, 4th revised edition (New York: HarperBusiness Essentials), chapter 8.

And our intuition tells us this can't happen. (Wealth is about economic resources, and trading doesn't create economic resources.) So, I view markets as being roughly efficient.[6]

I'll add one thought to the market efficiency debate. In recent years, I've come to think about what I call the efficiency chain—how prices are formed when financial assets are owned through several layers of intermediaries. Here's the idea. Say a mutual fund employs the smartest analysts who correctly calculate the value of every stock. But now the market drops. The fund's customers don't attempt to value the stocks in the fund or even the stock market. They get nervous and sell. The smart analysts then must sell to cover redemptions. Thus, fairly valued stocks can get cheap and cheap stocks can get cheaper. All the while, the smart people were acting smart.

The second point is that we won't need a separate way to value the stock apart from valuing the business. We're not going to care if the stock went up or down last month. We're not going to worry if it's January or not. We don't care what the options markets are saying. We don't care about a stock's beta. We're going to directly value the whole company, and the intrinsic value of a share will be the proportion of the value of the whole company it represents.

A share of stock represents a share of ownership in a company. If you own all the shares, you own the whole company. If a share price gets too far below the company's value, a person or other company will eventually buy all the shares to acquire the company. If the share price gets too far above the company's value, investors will spurn it and there will be no buyers to support the high price. A too-high price may also lead to investors shorting the stock. Shorting means selling shares you don't own with the hope of buying the stock back later at a lower price.

____

6   This characterization is used by Charlie Munger in his article "A Lesson on Elementary, Worldly Wisdom as It Relates to Investment Management & Business."

The third point is that there are no other sources of value outside of the cash flows a company generates. Whether a company pays dividends or buys back stock won't affect the valuation. Whether a company has a lot of cash won't matter. Doesn't cash have value? Yes, but if you buy the stock you can't reach in and grab the money. The cash has value in that it supports the company's business and the production of future earnings.

Is this approach the absolute chiseled-on-a-tablet-only-thing-that-works truth? No. If you can predict which companies will be taken over, you'll probably make out pretty good. If you can buy $50 million of computer equipment and hire a team of computer programmers, you might be able to make a lot in algorithmic market making. But the Straight Up Stock Investing approach does work, and it's something you can do with the resources you have.

To summarize, 1) we can value a company, 2) the value of a share only depends on the value of the company, and 3) the way we value a company only depends on its future cash flows.

Price/Earnings Ratio

As stated, we'll figure out the intrinsic value of a stock by determining the value of its future earnings stream. Then we'll compare the stock's price to its intrinsic value to determine if it's over or undervalued. A simple version of this model is the price/earnings ratio. You've probably heard of it. The price/earnings ratio is the stock's price divided by its earnings. It's what we'd pay for a dollar of this company's earnings. If the P/E ratio is 15, we're paying $15 for each dollar of earnings. In practice, earnings are either the trailing four quarter earnings or the estimate of the next year's earnings.

We can also turn the P/E ratio over to make it the earnings/price ratio. Say the P/E ratio is 15. If we invert it, we get 0.0667. In percentage terms, this is 6.67 percent, which is a useful way of stating this information because we have a sense for percentages. If this firm could just hand you its earnings every year, you'd earn 6.67 percent a year.

The problem with just stopping our analysis here is that we don't consider what earnings will be in the future, and that matters a lot. What if this year's earnings were bad because of an uncommon event, such as a recession? Then the P/E ratio would be high—because earnings would be low—and mislead us about the future. Plus, earnings tend to grow over time, and it seems like we should be incorporating this.

If you have an estimate for a company's long-term growth rate, you can make a rough adjustment to the earnings/price ratio to get the long-term rate of return:

$$r = e/p + g$$

You can think of e/p as the value component and g as the growth component. If you want to be a value investor, cover your right eye. If you want to be a growth investor, cover your left. But I recommend leaving both eyes open.

The trick here is that this is exactly true only for an infinite holding period.[7] So this formula can point you in the right direction, but you're going to want to do a more precise analysis, which we turn to next.

---

7   This formula can be gotten by rearranging the formula for the value of a
     perpetuity with growth:
     $P = e/(r−g)$

Discounted Cash Flow and Present Value

Question: Would you rather have a dollar today or a dollar in twenty years? Our gut tells us we'd rather have the dollar today. But why? Say the interest rate is 5 percent. We could invest our dollar today and in twenty years we'd have as follows:

$$\$1\times(1.05)^{20}=\$2.65$$

So we'd rather have that dollar today.

But if $1 today is worth $2.65 in the future, then $2.65 in future is worth $1 today, as inverting the above equation shows.

$$\$2.65/(1.05)^{20}=\$1$$

We say the *present value* of $2.65 twenty years from now is $1. This is the *discounted cash flow* method. This is the method we'll use for valuing companies. Repeat, **this is the method we'll use for valuing companies**. Each future year's earnings will be discounted back to the present. We'll add up the discounted cash flows, and that will be the value of the firm. We can then compare our value to the current market value to see if it is a bargain or not.

A way to think about it is that we must convert all those cash flows arriving at different times into a *common unit* so that we can combine them. We can't just mix quarts, cups, and gallons of water and know how much water we have. We need to convert to one unit, such as quarts. With money, our unit is dollars today. To convert gallons to quarts, we divide by four. To convert dollars arriving in the future to dollars today, we compute the present value.

Here's the formula. Remember, your spreadsheet will do this calculation for you.

$$IV = \sum_{t=1}^{T} \frac{CF_t}{(1+r)^t}$$

IV = intrinsic value, the present value of all future cash flows/earnings

CF = cash flow

r = discount rate

What is the appropriate discount rate? That is, what rate should we use to transport future cash flows to the present? This is a topic of endless discussion and uncertainty (and at least one Dilbert cartoon). A reasonable place to start is what stocks have returned over the long term. It varies by period, but over the last hundred years, stocks have returned a little over 10 percent[8] per year. This could be interpreted as investors have *required* a 10 percent return on stocks, suggesting 10 percent is a reasonable discount rate.

You could also consider the current level of interest rates. If interest rates are very low (as they are as I write this), maybe you'd settle for a rate lower than 10 percent.

You could consider risk. If you thought a company was riskier than average, you could use a higher discount rate (that is, you'd require a higher return for investing in this company). If you thought a company was less risky, you could use a lower interest rate. For Walmart, which has a stable grocery business, you might settle for a lower rate. Conversely, for Harley-Davidson, which sells a discretionary good to a small population, you might want a higher rate. However, I think it's

---

8   Robert Shiller's website, of Yale, provides the basic data for computing returns over various periods. www.econ.yale.edu/~shiller/

simpler to use the same discount rate for all companies and to focus on the difference between the real company worth and its share price.

If you think that a company's future cash flows are so uncertain that you're contemplating discount rates on the order of 15 percent or 20 percent, my suggestion is drop that company from consideration. It's probably too risky. You'll never find a company in which you are 100 percent certain in its future cash flows. But you will find plenty of companies in which you have some degree of confidence in what the path of future cash flows will look like. Stick with those companies.

In what follows, I'll use 10 percent for the discount rate.

Internal Rate of Return

One last concept before we start valuing stocks. The *internal rate of return* is the interest rate that makes the discounted value of the future cash flows equal to the current price. That is, in the above formula, if you know the price today and the future cash flows, you can solve for r.

$$P = \sum_{t=1}^{T} \frac{CF_t}{(1 + irr)^t}$$

In the restated formula, instead of solving for the intrinsic value, we just use the observed price (P) and solve for the interest rate (irr) that makes the discounted value of the future cash flows equal to that price.

Why is this useful? Because people naturally think of investment performance in terms of percentages. Thinking I'll earn 5 percent a year for twenty years is more intuitive than thinking if I invest a dollar today, I'll get $2.65 in twenty years. It's also a good complement to considering how over or undervalued a stock is. It's the same information, but it's useful to have a couple of perspectives.

Finally, if we base our decision on the internal rate of return, we don't have to come up with a discount rate. We can just evaluate the return, say 8 percent, and decide whether that's good enough or not. The uncertainty in choosing a discount rate hasn't disappeared. We've just moved it over to evaluating the return directly. For technical reasons, DCF and IRR are not the same. But for practical purposes they are. They will lead you to the same decisions.

Basic Model

Figure 4.1 presents the basic model. It's meant to implement the concepts we've discussed so far. We'll be extending it and making it more realistic as we progress. We will be valuing Flying Widget International (FWI), the world's premiere flying widget maker.

Let's dive in and work our way through the spreadsheet. We'll start with Flying Widget's earnings and end with its intrinsic value compared to its price.

Figure 4.1.

Flying Widget Int.		Discount-ed Cash Flow Method											
		years in future	1	2	3	4	5	6	7	8	9	10	future
	year 0	growth rate	5.00%	5.00%	5.00%	5.00%	5.00%	5.00%	5.00%	5.00%	5.00%	5.00%	5.00%
Cash Flow	$110.00	future cash flow	$115.50	$121.28	$127.34	$133.71	$140.39	$147.41	$154.78	$162.52	$170.65	$179.18	$188.14
		discount rate	10.00%	10.00%	10.00%	10.00%	10.00%	10.00%	10.00%	10.00%	10.00%	10.00%	
		dcf	$105.00	$100.23	$95.67	$91.32	$87.17	$83.21	$79.43	$75.82	$72.37	$69.08	
		sum of dcf 1-10	$859.30										
		dcf terminal value	$1,450.70										
		value of firm	$2,310.00		63%	← percentage of firm value from terminal value							
Shares outstanding	50	value per share	$46.20										
		price	$44.00										
		price/vps	95.24%										

Earnings

On the left side of Figure 1 is some basic information on FWI. In year 0, FWI earned $110 (the whole company) and had 50 shares outstanding. For now, we're going to use the terms *cash flow* and *earnings* interchangeably. In future chapters, we'll be distinguishing between the two.

Future Earnings

The top right of the figure shows the years in the future. We start at year 0, then go out one year, two years, and so on. Below each year is the growth rate of the earnings. We'll assume that earnings grow 5 percent each year. We don't know that, of course, and this is one of the numbers we'll have to put some thought into, but for this example we'll use 5 percent. If in year 0 the earnings are $110, in year 1 they will be 5 percent more, or $115.50. In year 2, they will be 5 percent higher than that, or $121.28. We'll also assume after year 10 earnings grow 5 percent a year.

Discounted Cash Flow

We'll go with a constant discount rate of 10 percent, about the long-term return of stocks. The DCF (discounted cash flow) row displays the future cash flow discounted back to the present. The present value of each individual future cash flow is given by the following formula:

$$PV_0(CF_t) = \frac{CF_t}{(1+r)^t}$$

Year 1's cash flow is discounted back one year. Year 2's is discounted back two years. And so on.

Sum of Discounted Cash Flows, Years 1–10

The first ten years of discounted cash flows are summed up to get $859.30. This would be the value of the firm if it only lasted ten years. But we're pretty sure that Flying Widget has a great future ahead of it.

Terminal Value

Let's assume that Flying Widget stays in business forever. We've computed the present value of the first ten years' worth of earnings. Now we need to compute the value of the earnings starting in year 11 and going on into eternity. Luckily, there's a formula to give us this value.

The value today of a firm that produces a cash flow next year of CF, that grows at rate *g*, with a discount rate of *r*, is as follows:

$$PV_0 = \frac{CF}{r - g}$$

In our example, we're computing the terminal value in year 10, which is as follows:

$$\frac{\$188.14}{0.1 - 0.05} = \$3762.80$$

We must discount that back ten years to today, which gives us $1,450.70.

Adding this to the sum of the discounted cash flows for years 1 to 10, we get the total value of the firm of $2,310.00.

Note that the terminal value makes up 63 percent of the total value of the firm. This is typical using this methodology to value firms. For companies whose earnings are expected to occur far out in the future, this percentage will be higher.

Value per Share

With 50 shares outstanding, this gives us a value per share of $46.20 ($2,310/50). If the price for a share on the stock market was $44.00, then the price divided by the value gives us about 0.95, meaning that FWI is trading at 95 percent of its intrinsic value, which is close to fair value.

The discount to fair value is only about 5 percent in this example, so we wouldn't be interested in buying it. I look for a discount of 40 percent, or when the stock is trading at 60 percent of fair value, before I consider buying it. Sixty percent of $46.20 is $27.12, so I could consider buying FWI if its price was $27.12 or less. (On the spreadsheet I maintain, companies priced at 60 percent or less of intrinsic value light up green.)

I admit the 60 percent is somewhat arbitrary. It's a level I've grown comfortable with and—to use a Graham/Buffett phrase—it provides a reasonable margin of safety. The hope is that when it's time to invest, you'll have several undervalued stocks to pick from. Then you can start with the cheapest and work your way up.

Internal Rate of Return

The internal rate of return presents the investment prospects of a stock, just as the discounted cash flow method does. However, in the case of the IRR, instead of producing a stock's fair value, we produce the average annual return we'd receive for holding the stock for a long time. The IRR uses the same information as DCF; it just produces a different output.

Figure 2 presents the internal rate of return calculation.

Figure 4.2.

Flying Widget Int.		Internal Rate of Return Method							
			5.00%	5.00%	5.00%	…	5.00%	5.00%	5.00%
	year 0	cost	**1**	**2**	**3**	…	**48**	**49**	**50**
Cash Flow	$110.00	-$2,200.00	$115.50	$121.28	$127.34	…	$1,144.14	$1,201.35	$3,461.41
Shares outstanding	50								
		IRR	9.71%						

As before, FWI earns $110.00 in year 0, has 50 shares outstanding, and grows earnings at 5 percent a year. To compute an internal rate of return using a spreadsheet, we need to have every single cash flow, both the outflows (what you pay) and the inflows (the earnings). The outflow is what you'd pay for the whole company in year 0. This is the share price times the number of shares, $44.00 × 50 = $2,200.00. (In your spreadsheet, this needs to be a negative number.) The inflows are the future earnings. Since we can't have an infinity of numbers, we'll just include the cash flows for many years. The earnings we leave out are in the distant future, with little present value, and won't have much of an effect whether we include them or not. We'll include the first fifty years' earnings. Since assuming the company ceases to exist after 50 years might make some of us uncomfortable, we'll assume we also get our $2200.00 back in year 50, though it only affects the result by about six basis points. (This is why the year 50 cash flow is $3,461.41, not $1,261.41) The internal rate of return is 9.71 percent. This is what you'd get for buying FWI at the current price and holding it a long time.

If the DCF method shows the stock price equal to fair value, then the IRR should be close to 10 percent, since 10 percent is the discount rate we used in the DCF calculation. It won't be exact, since we are assuming different time periods and the methodologies differ slightly, but it will be close.

Summary

- Companies can be valued.

- The value of a share is the proportion ownership of the company it represents.

- The value of a company depends on its future cash flows.

- To compute the intrinsic value of a company, use the discounted cash flow method.

- Consider buying stocks that are priced at a significant discount to their intrinsic value.

- The internal rate of return is also a useful measure to compute.

Chapter 5:
THE EXPANDED MODEL

In this chapter, we're going to expand the basic model to move it closer to reality. First, we'll talk about the difference between reported earnings and cash flows and why it's important. Then we'll move on to cash flow smoothing and what growth rate to assume for cash flows. Finally, we'll analyze a real company, Union Pacific, to illustrate these concepts.

Cash Flows vs. Earnings

As an investor, what you care about is how much money a company makes that it can distribute to you (even if it chooses to invest it on your behalf). Money that is free and clear. This can be the same amount a firm reports on its income statement, but it isn't necessarily. And it's important to understand the difference. To understand this difference, we have to take a brief detour into accounting.

When someone uses the word *earnings* in the context of a company's financial performance, they're usually referring to the company's accounting earnings, or more technically, the firm's GAAP earnings. (GAAP stands for *generally accepted accounting principles*.) This is the number at the bottom of a firm's income statement.

GAAP earnings are based on accrual accounting, the principle that revenues and expenses should be recognized when a transaction binds the parties, not necessarily when the cash changes hands. Accounting policy makers believe this gives the most accurate representation of a firm's financial position. Broadly speaking, it does. But ultimately an investor cares about how much cash a company will generate going forward, and this requires a deeper dive. We'll need to consider depreciation and capital expenditures.

Say Flying Widget International buys a widget-making machine for $100 in 2020. You might think that FWI would take that $100 as an expense in 2020. But that isn't how GAAP accounting works. (I'm going to have to throw around some accounting terms, so please bear with me. We will be talking more about financial statements in chapter 7.) The GAAP thought process is, yes, you disburse $100 for the machine, but then you have the machine, which is a long-lived asset worth $100. So, you've just exchanged one asset, cash, for another, the widget-making machine. It's like trading an airplane for a boat. You really haven't gained or lost anything; it's just that the assets you own look different.

Here's another example. Say you pay $500,000 cash for a house. Has your wealth declined by $500,000? No. You have $500,000 less in cash, but you now have the house, which is worth $500,000. Your wealth (the value of all your assets) is unchanged.

Now machines do wear down over time, and GAAP recognizes this. Under GAAP—and here's the key point—the firm expenses the purchase of the machine a little bit at a time as it progresses through its useful life, not when the cash is put out. This wearing down over time is called *depreciation*. What is the useful life of a piece of equipment or a building? Of course, we can't know for certain, so the accounting authorities provide schedules to use. They're best guesses, but you must use something.

Let's say the widget-making machine has a useful life of ten years. When FWI first purchases the machine it is at full strength, but after ten years it can no longer produce anything and needs to be replaced. If you tried to sell it, no one would give you anything. (See Figure 5.1.) Over the course of ten years, Flying Widget takes an expense of $10 each year. But here's the thing: That $10 a year expense doesn't involve any cash going out the door. It's recognizing cash that went out the door in a previous year. So, the firm still has the $10 to do something with, like pay a dividend or invest in a new project.

Figure 5.1.

Year	Purchase machine	Expense on income statement	Uses cash?	Accounting value of machine
0	$100	$0	Yes	$100
1		$10	No	$90
2		$10	No	$80
3		$10	No	$70
4		$10	No	$60
5		$10	No	$50
6		$10	No	$40
7		$10	No	$30
8		$10	No	$20
9		$10	No	$10
10		$10	No	$0

Sometimes finance professionals will define cash flow as GAAP earnings plus depreciation. The logic is that depreciation doesn't involve cash going out the door, so just reverse that expense. Now you can probably already see the problem here. Yes, depreciation represents a noncash expense for past capital expenditures, but FWI will have to buy new equipment at some point to replace the equipment that is wearing out. And that capital expenditure will require cash out the door.

For a typical industrial firm, over the long-term, capital expenditures and depreciation expense should be about the same. That is, the cumulated depreciation should give a decent picture of how much money a firm needs to replace its fixed assets. But not always, and it's this combination of depreciation and capital expenditure that can drive a wedge between reported earnings and cash available to the owners. It can go either way. Let's consider some examples.

For some companies, like financial firms, little plant, property, and equipment is required to run the business. For companies like this, simply using earnings is probably fine. When I analyze a bank, I generally just ignore depreciation and capital expenditure. Sometimes I can't even find it on their financial statements.

If a company has made big capital investments in the past but doesn't need much capex going forward, then GAAP earnings will understate cash available to owners. An example might be the purchase of a building. Everyday maintenance, such as servicing a furnace, will show up as an expense on the income statement. In general, depreciation expense has a big effect on the financial results of the real estate industry. Since real estate projects don't require much capital expenditure, they can produce significant cash flow even when reported earnings are zero.

The case you need to be on the watch for is when a company must continually invest in fixed assets just to maintain its business and the assets it needs to buy increase in price over time. If the cost of equipment is going up, a company will be expensing equipment it bought years ago at historical prices but buying new equipment at today's prices. In this case, reported earnings will overstate the cash available to the owners.

Here's the working definition of cash flow we'll be using:

Cash Flow = GAAP earnings + Depreciation – PPE

We start with net income, add back depreciation, and subtract out the actual cash expenditure on plant, property, and equipment (PPE).

Figure 5.2.

Union Pacific			
	Average 2007 - 2020		
net income	depreciation	PPE	cash flow
$4,473	$1,819	$3,294	$2,999
Source: Firm's financial statements. Author's calculations.			

As an example, let's look at Union Pacific, the railroad company. Figure 5.2 presents the average net income (GAAP earnings), depreciation expense, plant property and equipment expenditure, and the cash flow for the years 2007 through 2020. Over this fourteen-year period, average net income was $4.47 billion dollars. Average depreciation was $1.82 billion. You might think, "Great!" because the net income number understates the cash I received by $1.82 billion. But not so fast. Over the same period, Union Pacific spent $3.29 billion on capital expenditures, $1.46 billion more than the depreciation expense. Over this fourteen-year period, the average cash available to shareholders, about $3 billion, was considerably less than reported earnings, $4.47 billion.

As it turns out, if you look at Union Pacific's financials, you'll see that in every year PPE expenditure was bigger than depreciation. It takes a lot of capital expenditure to keep a railroad running! This suggests that available cash will be less than reported earnings going forward. Since the cash is what you get, you'll want to use this cash flow number to compute your valuations, not earnings.

A caution here, you need to compare apples to apples. You must compare capital expenditure to depreciation for previous capital expenditures. Sometimes firms will lump other items into depreciation and other items into capital expenditures. Or sometimes they will break things out into other lines. You want to try to work through that to pair up depreciation to the stuff that is being depreciated. It isn't always easy.

The lesson is that you want to use cash flow, not just reported earnings. A good way to define cash flow is to start with earnings, add back the noncash expense depreciation, and then subtract out the actual cash used for capital expenditures.

Unfortunately for us investors, there is a circus parade of noncash expenses and revenues. Impairment of an asset's value is one. It can get complicated, and ultimately you just have to make decisions about how you treat some things. Usually, if a noncash charge is small, I'll just ignore it.

At this point, one could criticize the model we are building by pointing out how all these other noncash expenses could throw off the accuracy of this simple measure of cash flow. My response is that's a fair criticism. But as the saying goes: All models are wrong, but some are useful.[9] We're building something useful.

Another adjustment to free cash flow you'll sometimes see is change in working capital. Working capital is cash a business needs on hand to operate. In your lemonade stand, it's the roll of quarters you had to keep on hand to make change. The idea is that as a company grows it needs more cash on hand to run its business. Therefore, some of the cash a business generates is not available but must be held. In my experience, this number isn't that big and isn't that relevant to large companies with access to capital. So we're just going to ignore it.

Smoothing Cash Flows

Our calculation of a firm's intrinsic value is a function of its future cash flows. To estimate future cash flows, we usually apply a growth rate

---

9   This statement is generally attributed to statistician George Box.

to current cash flows. But what if last year was a recession year? Then the most recent annual earnings might be temporarily weak. Or what if the firm made a big, one-time capital expenditure? Cash flows can bounce around for all sorts of reasons. We want to apply our cash flow growth rate to a measure of earnings that is representative of current circumstances.

To smooth out possible bumps, I recommend using a three-year average of the most recent annual cash flows. There is an arbitrary component to this, I admit. Two years is too short because it's common for a disruption, such as a recession, to overlap portions of two calendar years, but much less likely to span three. The longer you go out, say four of five years, the greater the chance the company's circumstances will have changed in a meaningful way. Of course, if expanding to four years is just what it takes to smooth out the effects of a change in tax law, or shortening to two years drops the years before a game-changing new product, then go ahead and do that. But three years seems reasonable, and that will be our default in what follows.

Figure 5.3.

Flying Widget Int.	2018	2019	2020
net income	$100.00	$105.00	$110.00
depreciation	17.15	18.86	20.75
PPE	21.44	23.58	25.94
cash flow	$95.71	$100.28	$104.81
average 3-year cash flow			$100.27

years in future	1	2	3	...	9	10	future
growth rate	5.00%	5.00%	5.00%	...	5.00%	5.00%	5.00%
cash flow	$105.28	$110.55	$116.07		$155.55	$163.33	$171.50
discount rate	10.00%	10.00%	10.00%		10.00%	10.00%	
dcf	$95.71	$91.36	$87.21		$65.97	$62.97	
sum of dcf	$783.29						
dcf terminal value	$1,322.38						
value of firm	$2,105.67						
value per share	$42.11						
price	$44.00						
price/vps	104.48%						

Figure 5.3 displays the expanded valuation for Flying Widget International. There are two changes from the basic model of chapter 4. First, earnings are just the starting point to get to cash flow, which then drives the valuation. In 2020, FWI's earnings are $110.00. We add back in depreciation of $20.75 and then subtract out PPE of $25.94, leaving a cash flow of $104.81. Second, we smooth the cash flows over three years, which yields $100.27. Using a growth rate of 5 percent, this gives an estimate of next year's cash flow of $105.28.

Growth Rate

The growth rate of a company's cash flows has a big impact on the valuation. So we want to put some thought into it. What growth rate should we use? In Figure 5.3, we've just assumed a cash flow growth rate of 5 percent, but where does that come from? A separate but related question is this: What should we use for the terminal rate of growth—the rate we assume the company will grow at far into the future? In this section, we'll address companies with normal rates of growth. In the next chapter, we'll discuss how to handle companies with exceptional cash flow growth.

The first place to start is always your own research. If you've been studying Flying Widget and the whole widget industry, and you've concluded that it's going to grow 8 percent a year for the next four years, then use 8 percent a year for the next four years. Keep in mind, even great companies' earnings will revert to lower rates at some point in the future. However, there is no symmetry for bad companies. Their earnings can stay low forever.

A second good place to start is with a firm's recent growth rate. If a firm has been growing earnings consistently at 7 percent a year, then it's reasonable to assume 7 percent earnings growth for at least a few years out. Of course, you can combine recent earnings growth with other results of your research to arrive at your estimate of earnings growth. Say your company has had that 7 percent growth rate but is about to introduce some great new products. Maybe you build off 7 percent to get to 10 percent.

A third approach is to use Wall Street analysts' forecasts for the near term. If every analyst is forecasting that Flying Widget will make $105 next year, you could adjust your growth rate to produce $105. For short horizons, analysts' earnings forecasts are pretty good. (Price forecasts are another matter.)

What if you're kind of not sure? Maybe you're following a company because you think it's solid and could be undervalued, but you don't really have any special insights into its earnings future other than that you think it will enjoy reasonable growth along with the overall economy. This happens a lot. Take a bank such as Bank of America or Truist. Or take most any big bank for that matter. Most of these banks are well run, and their business models (borrow at low rates, lend at higher rates) are the same. There are ways they try to differentiate themselves, but most of their success is going to be a function of how the banking industry is doing. (With companies like these, you usually make your money by getting in at a good price, not by big growth.)

In situations like this, assuming earnings will grow at about the overall rate of the economy is reasonable. The Congressional Budget Office (CBO) in their 2020 Long-Term Budget Outlook estimates annual GDP growth from 2020–2050 to be 3.5 percent a year. Note that this is nominal GDP. Real growth is 1.6 percent, and 1.9 percent is inflation. When you read about GDP growth in the paper, it's generally real GDP that is reported.

You could also plug in the long-term growth rate for earnings. Using the data from Professor Robert Shiller's website[10], over the past one hundred

---

10   www.econ.yale.edu/~shiller/

years, from 1920 to 2020, earnings have grown about 5 percent a year. The starting point matters, so if you pick a different starting point you might get a different number. But if you use a long period, you'll end up in that area.

I usually use 5 percent, which I break down to 3 percent real growth and 2 percent inflation. This is a little more generous than the CBO. I justify it with natural optimism and a belief that the companies I follow will in the event do a little better than the overall economy.

The final growth rate we need is the long-term growth rate—what earnings growth will be after the first ten years. The good news is that we've already provided answers for this question. Any of the rates we've discussed above are reasonable: the CBO forecast, the earnings growth from the Shiller data set, or 5 percent. If you have a different forecast, that's fine too. I just caution not to pick one that's too big. If you really think your company is going to have high growth for twenty years, extend the model out to twenty years, then pick some GDP-like growth rate from that point onward.

The Power of Growth

People generally underestimate the power even low rates of growth have on long-term returns. Say you buy a bond for $100, with a $5 coupon, that matures in 100 years. Your return is 5 percent a year. Now say you buy the same bond, but now that $5 coupon grows at 5 percent a year. What's your annual return now? 10 percent. That's twice as big. In the bond (fixed coupon) scenario, 100 years of $5 coupons adds up to $500. In the 5 percent growth scenario, the sum of the coupons is $13,050— twenty-six times bigger.

We saw the formula in chapter 4, and it bears repeating:

$$e/p + g = r$$

Over the long-term, your return, r, equals the earnings yield plus the growth rate of earnings. An important caveat is that *long-term* technically means *infinite*. In the previous example, if the bond matured in twenty-five years, your annual return would be about 8 percent.

The point is that earnings growth makes a big difference. That's why a high P/E stock with a high rate of earnings growth can be a better investment than a low P/E stock with a low rate of earnings growth. This simple formula also shows why it doesn't make sense to think of value and growth as separate categories. The return is equal to value (E/P) plus growth (g).

A long-standing puzzle in the academic investing world is why stocks return so much more than bonds, even after accounting for risk. Part of the answer is people have difficulty getting their heads around the importance of growth.

Summary

1. Use cash flow, not accounting earnings.

2. Get a more stable estimate of current earnings power by smoothing cash flows over three years.

3. Estimate cash flow growth. Make sure your long-term growth rate isn't too big.

Chapter 6:
HIGH-GROWTH COMPANIES

In our basic and expanded models, we've forecast cash flows through a cash flow growth rate. That is, next year's cash flow is estimated by the product of this year's cash flow and the growth rate. This approach works well for companies that have current earnings. But it works poorly for companies that produce little earnings today but are expected to produce big earnings and big earnings growth in the future. In this chapter, we'll deal with companies that don't have earnings today but are expected to in the future.

A note on nomenclature: *Growth stock* is not a well-defined term. People use it in different ways. Sometimes it just means tech stocks. Sometimes it means stocks with high price/earnings ratios. Sometimes the definer is interested in value stocks, and growth stocks are whatever isn't a value stock. And sometimes it means stocks that are actually experiencing high earnings growth. The nomenclature doesn't really matter. What we're going to address in this chapter is how to value companies with little or no earnings today that are expected to have strong earnings in the future.

Figure 6.1.

Unity	2018	2019	2020	2021	Manually fill in years 1 - 10	1	2	3	4	5	6	7	8	9	10	future
	000's	(sim-plified numbers)														
									implied growth rates							
									25%	25%	26%	19%	20%	16%	15%	6%
net income	-131000	-163,000	-282,000	-532,000		0	0	250,000	312,500	390,000	490,000	585,000	700,000	810,000	930,000	985,800
depreciation																
PPE					discount rate	10.00%	10.00%	10.00%	10.00%	10.00%	10.00%	10.00%	10.00%	10.00%	10.00%	
cash flow	-131,000	-163,000	-282,000	-532,000	dcf	$0	$0	$187,829	$213,442	$242,159	$276,592	$300,197	$326,555	$343,519	$358,555	
					sum of dcf	$2,248,849										
					dcf terminal value	$9,501,714										
shares out-standing		114,442	169,973	340,000	value of firm	$11,750,563		percent-age from terminal value:			81%					
					value per share	$34.56										
					price	$105.00										
					price/vps	303.82%										

As our high growth company, we'll use Unity, a maker of software used to design video games (a game engine). Unity went public in 2020. Its financial information is shown in Figure 6.1. To simplify things, I left out the depreciation and capital expenditure, so go to Unity's financial statements if you'd like all the details.

Video games are a booming business, growing by leaps and bounds. So, it's plausible that a company that helps people make video games will make a lot of money. But companies that are starting out often need to spend a lot to get the company up and running. Even for a great product, it often takes time to create awareness. For instance, Airbnb was founded way back in 2008, but most people didn't hear of it until much later. Of course, some companies never make money; that, too, happens all the time. But let's assume that Unity is one of those companies that loses money early in its life and then starts making money.

As seen in Figure 6.1, Unity has only ever lost money. At the beginning of 2022, management forecast a small loss for all of 2022. So right away, forecasting earnings off a growth rate is a problem. A big growth rate times a negative number is going to be a bigger negative number, so we'll have to approach it a different way.

Instead, we'll leave the growth rate out and estimate the earnings directly. That is, we'll estimate what earnings will be for the next few years without using the company's financial history.

This can be a tough problem—it's easier to estimate a growth rate of earnings than the earnings themselves. But you have some places to turn. Sometimes firms will provide estimates. For instance, Unity says it plans to be profitable in 2023. Wall Street analysts' forecasts are also a good source. Analysts' stock price forecasts are not very accurate, but near-term earnings forecasts are. And as always, you can do your own research.

For example, say you have an estimate of how many cars Tesla is going to sell next year; you could start with that and work back. How? A simple way would be to 1) find how many cars Tesla sold this year; 2) find how much revenue and expense these sales generated; 3) assume next year's revenue and expense will increase in proportion to car sales; and 4) compute next year's profit. Simple, yes, but it moves you in the right direction and could be the starting point for a more detailed analysis.

For the Unity example, I've chosen reasonable but speculative numbers. I estimate that Unity will earn $250 million in 2024 and then grow 25 percent a year, with the growth rate slowly drifting down to 6 percent. Discounting back at 10 percent produces a value per share of about $35. Since the price of a share is $105, the shares are overvalued by a lot. Of course, this number could be way off. If Unity starts earning billions soon, it's undervalued. The point is to show the methodology of picking the initial earnings number directly, bypassing an earnings growth rate. In this example, once I have the initial base earnings, I switch over to using a growth rate, but I could have continued estimating the earnings number directly.

Sometimes with hot growth stocks, investors don't bother to explore whether any plausible future earnings support the current price. I caution against this. If you think future earnings will be huge, fine. Maybe the company will take over the whole industry. Fine. Put those numbers into the model and see what intrinsic value you get. If even the most extraordinary earnings imaginable lead to an overvaluation, be wary.

Now you personally might want to buy a growth stock because you think others will bid it up further or because you think a bigger company will buy it. And you may be right. Maybe Microsoft will buy Unity someday. If you can predict those things, you don't need this book. But my advice to you is this: If you can't come up with any reasonable estimates for earnings that justify the current stock price, just pass and wait for something else.

For great companies, tremendous earnings growth early in their lives is possible. But over time, growth rates will slow, even for great companies. If a company earns a million dollars and it doubles earnings every year, in ten years it will earn about a billion dollars. But in twenty years it will earn about a trillion dollars. The entire U.S. economy is around $20 trillion.

Summary

- For companies that are expected to grow but don't have earnings today, you'll need to estimate the first few years' earnings directly, rather than estimating the growth rate.

- Be wary if even very optimistic earnings forecasts can't support the current stock price.

- High growth can't be maintained forever.

Chapter 7:
READING FINANCIAL STATEMENTS

In this chapter we'll talk about financial statements, what information we need from them, and where to find it. A firm's financial statements are a trove of information. As part of your research, you'll want to go over them in depth. But for our present purposes, we're just going to gather the information we need to populate our valuation spread sheet. We need four numbers: 1) net income; 2) depreciation; 3) plant property and equipment (capital expenditure); and 4) shares outstanding. Keeping with our example, we'll examine the financial statements of Union Pacific.

There are three basic financial statements that firms are required to produce: income statement, balance sheet, and statement of cash flows. The numbers we need are presented on the income statement and the statement of cash flows. The firm's accountant compiles these numbers and presents them according to Generally Accepted Accounting Principles (GAAP). These statements are always found in a company's 10-K, its annual filing with the SEC, and companies will often make them available in other ways, such as on the investor relations section of their website.

The income statement presents a firm's revenues and expenses, the net of which is a firm's earnings. As you'll recall, the principle is that revenues and expenses are recognized when the parties enter a binding transaction, not necessarily when the cash changes hands. Say a boat maker delivers a boat to a customer and gives them thirty days to pay. The boat maker would record the revenue when it delivers, even if the payment is received later. (On the balance sheet, an accounts receivable entry would take the place of cash.)

The balance sheet presents what a firm owns and owes (assets and liabilities) at a point in time. How much cash does a firm have on hand, how much equipment does it own, how much debt does it have? We don't need any numbers from the balance sheet for our spreadsheet, but it presents a lot of important information you'll want to investigate for the companies you follow. For instance, how much debt a firm has is on the balance sheet.

If you subtract the liabilities from the assets, what's left is shareholders' equity—what the shareholders own free and clear. Dividing this by shares outstanding yields book value per share. Book value per share is not as useful a measure as it once was. One reason is that today, firms' earnings are increasingly connected to intangibles—a brand, a network—which book value often misses. Another reason is the prevalence of share repurchases, which tend to push down book value per share. Book value per share can be useful for analyzing some companies, such as banks, where earnings are more connected to earnings accumulated over the years and less to intangibles.

The statement of cash flows is exactly what it sounds like. It tracks the cash coming in and out over the reporting period. For instance, if a company spends cash on a major capital investment, you'll see it here, even though it does not show up on the income statement (because it's just exchanging one asset for another). If a company writes down an asset but no cash goes out the door, the statement of cash flows will let you know. You'll also find items such as dividends and stock repurchases. We'll be using the statement of cash flows to get depreciation and capital expenditures.

After presenting the basic financial statements, the 10-K will present the Notes to the financial statements. If there is something in the standard financial statements you can't understand, the Notes are the first place to look. If you can't quite figure out what a firm is lumping into its depreciation and amortization number, you might find it broken out in a note.

Finding the Financial Statements

First, go to the investor relations section of the Union Pacific website. Typing "Union Pacific Investor Relations" into your search engine will do the trick. Next, find its most recent 10-K. As I write this, it's late 2021, so the most recent 10-K is for the year 2020. The 10-K is the report of a firm's operations that must be filed with the Securities and Exchange Commission (SEC) every year. The 10-Q is what they file quarterly. Almost all firms produce an annual report for shareholders. The information we need can usually be found in that too. Note that most companies end their financial years on December 31, but not all do. It often takes firms a couple of months after their fiscal year ends to file their 10-K.

In the table of contents, find Item 8 (it's Item 8 for all companies). This will direct you to the financial statements section of the filing. Here you will find the income statement, balance sheet, statement of cash flows, and much more financial information.

Union Pacific Example

The income statement for Union Pacific is presented in Figure 7.1. The first number we need for our spreadsheet is net income, which is $5.349 billion.

The second number we need from the income statement is the shares outstanding. Usually, the firm will present the average number of shares outstanding in the year. Strictly speaking, you'd prefer the number of shares at the end of the year, but I usually go with the weighted average number. However, if the firm had a big share issuance, you'd want to get the end-of-year number. Firms also usually present a "diluted" version of shares outstanding. This number assumes anything that can be converted to common shares, such as stock options and warrants, has been converted. These conversions result in a bigger share count and is therefore more conservative, so I go with that.

Occasionally a firm won't report the shares outstanding on the income statement. When this is the case, you'll have to search the Notes section. Usually there is a note called "Earnings per Share," and it's there.

The balance sheet presents the assets and liabilities of a company as of the end of the firm's reporting period. We don't need any of these numbers for our spreadsheet, but it's a good idea to look through them. One worthwhile comparison to make is how much debt a company has relative to its assets. If debt seems too high, you may want to dig deeper—especially if the business is cyclical. Union Pacific has about $26 billion in long-term debt compared to about $62 billion in assets at the end of 2020. That's a ratio of about forty percent, which doesn't bother me. If the ratio were seventy or eighty percent, I'd get concerned that a recession may put Union Pacific in a tough position.

Note the balance sheet is static. It presents the assets and liabilities of a firm at a fixed point in time. The income statement and statement of cash flows presents the flow of economic activity over a year. For instance, the income statement gives you how much income was earned from January 1 through December 31.

Figure 7.1.

CONSOLIDATED STATEMENTS OF INCOME
Union Pacific Corporation and Subsidiary Companies

Millions. Except Per Share Amounts, for the Years Ended December 31,		2020		2019		2018
Operating revenues:						
Freight revenues	$	18,251	$	20,243	$	21,384
Other revenues		1,282		1,465		1,448
Total operating revenues		19,533		21,708		22,832
Operating expenses:						
Compensation and benefits		3,993		4,533		5,056
Depreciation		2,210		2,216		2,191
Purchased services and materials		1,962		2,254		2,443
Fuel		1,314		2,107		2,531
Equipment and other rents		875		984		1,072
Other		1,345		1,060		1,022
Total operating expenses		11,699		13,154		14,315
Operating income		7,834		8,554		8,517
Other income (Note 6)		287		243		94
Interest expense		(1,141)		(1,050)		(870)
Income before income taxes		6,980		7,747		7,741
Income tax expense (Note 7)		(1,631)		(1,828)		(1,775)
Net income	$	5,349	$	5,919	$	5,966
Share and Per Share (Note 8):						
Earnings per share - basic	$	7.90	$	8.41	$	7.95
Earnings per share - diluted	$	7.88	$	8.38	$	7.91
Weighted average number of shares - basic		677.3		703.5		750.9
Weighted average number of shares - diluted		679.1		706.1		754.3

Source: Union Pacific Corporation, Form 10-K, SEC filing for fiscal year ended December 31st, 2020

As we discussed in chapter 5, we want to adjust net income to account for a firm's cash outlay on PPE and for depreciation. PPE requires cash but is not an expense on the income statement. Depreciation does not require cash but is an expense on the income statement. If past capital expenditure is different from future capital expenditure, then net income can be an inaccurate indicator of the cash that will be available to owners in the future.

PPE and depreciation are both presented on the statement of cash flows, as shown in Figure 7.2.

Looking at Union Pacific's cash flow statement, we see the depreciation number is $2.21 billion. Since this is an expense that doesn't involve cash, we add it back to net income. The line "Capital Investments" is capex. This is the cash that was actually spent on PPE in 2020. So we further subtract that out to arrive at our measure of cash flow.

Figure 7.2.

CONSOLIDATED STATEMENTS OF CASH FLOWS
Union Pacific Corporation and Subsidiary Companies

Millions, for the Years Ended December 31,	2020	2019	2018
Operating Activities			
Net income	$ 5,349	$ 5,919	$ 5,966
Adjustments to reconcile net income to cash provided by operating activities:			
Depreciation	2,210	2,216	2,191
Deferred and other income taxes	340	566	338
Net gain on non-operating asset dispositions	(115)	(20)	(30)
Other operating activities, net	490	98	347
Changes in current assets and liabilities:			
Accounts receivable, net	90	160	(262)
Materials and supplies	113	(9)	7
Other current assets	(34)	87	(24)
Accounts payable and other current liabilities	(73)	(179)	(125)
Income and other taxes	170	(229)	278
Cash provided by operating activities	8,540	8,609	8,686
Investing Activities			
Capital investments	(2,927)	(3,453)	(3,437)
Proceeds from asset sales	149	74	63
Maturities of short-term investments (Note 13)	141	130	90
Purchases of short-term investments (Note 13)	(136)	(115)	(90)
Other investing activities, net	97	(71)	(37)
Cash used in investing activities	(2,676)	(3,435)	(3,411)
Financing Activities			
Debt issued (Note 14)	4,004	3,986	6,892
Share repurchase programs (Note 18)	(3,705)	(5,804)	(8,225)
Dividends paid	(2,626)	(2,598)	(2,299)
Debt repaid	(2,053)	(817)	(1,736)
Debt exchange	(328)	(387)	-
Net issuance of commercial paper (Note 14)	(127)	(6)	194
Other financing activities, net	(67)	(20)	(48)
Cash used in financing activities	(4,902)	(5,646)	(5,222)
Net change in cash, cash equivalents, and restricted cash	962	(472)	53
Cash, cash equivalents, and restricted cash at beginning of year	856	1,328	1,275
Cash, cash equivalents, and restricted cash at end of year	$ 1,818	$ 856	$ 1,328

Source: Union Pacific Corporation, Form 10-K, SEC filing for fiscal year ended December 31st, 2020

Here's the formula again:

Cash Flow = GAAP earnings + Depreciation – PPE

$4,632 = $5,349 + $2,210–$2,927

As we can see, Union Pacific spent more on capital expenditure in 2020 than it took as a depreciation expense for previous capital expenditure: $2.93 billion versus $2.21 billion. So its cash flow is lower than its net income. This is typical for the railroad industry. Keeping the trains running requires massive capital expenditure. And because of inflation, the new equipment you must buy is more expensive than the past capital expenditures that you are expensing (depreciating).

Now, it would be wonderful if we could end the discussion here. But unfortunately, the world of corporate finance and investing is a lot more complicated. There are lots of other expenditures that don't require cash and lots more items that require cash but don't show up on the income statement. I can't give you an algorithm that determines how to deal with every situation. You'll have to make your own assessments. If you're not sure what's going on with a reported item, try looking through the Notes to the financial statements. You may find guidance there.

Here's one tip: If the item you're contemplating is small, just ignore it. No use spending your valuable time on items that won't have an impact on your analysis.

A write-down of an asset is an item you'll often see. For instance, in 2015 ATT bought DirecTV for $68 billion. DirecTV provides satellite TV services, and as people moved to streaming over the internet, these assets lost value. In 2021, ATT wrote DirecTV down by $15.5 billion. No cash was involved, it was just a recognition that DirecTV was then worth less than ATT paid for it. So, what do you?

It's a big number, so it can't be ignored. What we really care about are future cash flows. That's our whole philosophy. If a company adjusted an asset's valuation, but our estimate of future cash flows did not change, our valuation of the company would not change.

However, if a company revalues a major asset, that could be a signal that you should revisit your earnings projections. A big impairment is never a good sign and could signal that management thinks that business will not be as good as previously thought.

In the ATT case, I would probably add back the write-down to earnings but then reevaluate the estimates of future earnings. Maybe they need to be reduced if earnings I had been counting on will no longer be there.

Again, there will always be noncash expenses and revenues to consider. You're going to have to make decisions on how to handle them. You may not get the perfect answer, but if you at least try to work toward cash flow, you'll be moving in the right direction.

Summary

1. The principle financial statements are the income statement, the balance sheet, and the statement of cash flows.

2. These statements are easy to find online by going to the investor relations section of a company's website.

3. The numbers we need are as follows: 1) net income; 2) depreciation; 3) plant, property, and equipment (capital expenditure); and 4) shares outstanding.

PART III: PERSONALIZATION

Chapter 8:
RISK MANAGEMENT

If our analysis shows that a stock should earn a 10 percent annual return for ten years, wouldn't it be great if our stock earned exactly 10 percent in each of the ten years? Seems fair, right? But we know markets don't work this way. We may get to 10 percent by earning 5 percent one year and 15 percent another. Or 0 percent one year and 20 percent another.

Of course, it could be worse. We may not get a 10 percent annual return at all. Maybe we earn more. But maybe we earn less. And this chance of earning less is what we call *risk*.

I define risk as *the probability of taking a big loss*.

It's the chance that something really bad happens. That you will lose a lot or all your money. It's not just that you won't achieve your expected return. Expecting to earn 10 percent but achieving only 9 percent isn't the notion we're after. Just getting your money back is a zero return, but it isn't the end of the world. Risk is the probability that you will lose a lot of money.

Of course, there are lots of ways to lose money. Therefore, it's hard to come up with a single risk management tool that always protects you. Actually, there is one. And that's to never make a risky investment. Keep your money in cash or Treasury bills. Of course, if you do that, you'll never make any money either.

Let's review a few of the standard ways of thinking about risk before we get to the one I recommend.

Volatility

If you've taken a finance class, you're probably familiar with the term *volatility*. Volatility is the tendency to change quickly and unpredictably. (Yes, I got that definition from the dictionary.) Consider stock A and stock B. Let's assume that the distribution of their future returns looks like this:

Figure 8.1.

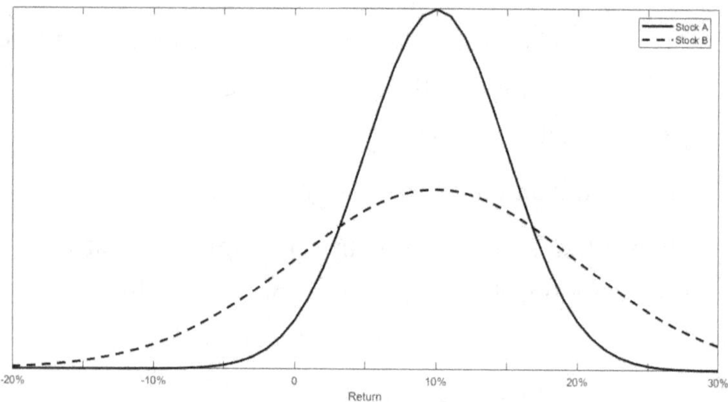

In both cases, you expect to earn 10 percent, but B's returns are more disperse. A's distribution of returns is tighter around 10 percent. A big loss, say a loss of 10 percent, is more likely with B than A. We say that B is more volatile than A.

Volatility is one way of quantifying risk. In standard financial theory, people are risk averse—they dislike big losses more than they like big gains. Losing $1,000 feels worse than making $1,000 feels good. Therefore, volatility is bad. For a given expected return, you'd like as little volatility as possible.

Volatility is an important concept, and it's good to be familiar with it, but we're not going to emphasize it here. One reason is that most stock portfolios you put together are going to end up having similar volatilities.

Leverage

Leverage is how much a firm has borrowed relative to what the owners have contributed. Leverage amplifies returns, both on the upside and the downside, which is why it's related to risk.

Say firm A has $10 in equity capital. That is, its owners put up $10. It invests in a project that can either make 10 percent or lose 10 percent. If the project makes 10 percent, the owners earn a return of $10 × 10 percent = $1, and now have $11. If they lose 10 percent, they lose $1 and are left with $9.

Figure 8.2.

	equity	debt	total capital	final equity	
				10%	-10%
firm A	$10.00	$0	$10.00	$11.00	$9.00
firm B	$10.00	$90.00	$100.00	$20.00	$0.00

Now consider firm B. Like A, it has $10 of equity capital, but it also borrows $90 for total capital of $100. It's leveraged 9 to 1. B invests its capital in the same project as A. If the project returns 10 percent, the equity holders get $100 × 10 percent = $10. Including the original $10 leaves them a total of $20. In other words, they've doubled their money. But if the project comes up tails and they lose 10 percent, they lose $10. Since $10 is all the equity (and they'd owe some interest on the debt), they've lost the company. If things go bad, A lives to fight another day while B does not.

Note how leverage increases volatility. Firm A can make $1 or lose $1. Firm B can make $10 or lose $10. Because of leverage, firm B is more volatile than firm A. Leverage and volatility go hand in hand. Whenever you borrow to fund an investment, you increase the upside as well as the downside.

By the way, if you assume the year is 2008 and substitute "GE corporation" for firm B, you get a good idea of why we don't hear much about GE these days. GE (General Electric), for most of its history, made industrial and consumer products. Over time, they increased the size of their financing business, which involved using their size to borrow at low rates and lend at high rates. As things went well, GE expanded its lending business. When the 2008 recession hit, the firms GE lent to had trouble paying GE back. This put GE at risk of not being able to pay back *its* lenders, which could have bankrupted the firm. It was only then that people realized just how levered GE had become.[11]

Back in 2008, the banking industry had much higher leverage than today. When the economy weakened, many banks found themselves on the brink and had to be bailed out by the Federal Reserve. At the end of 2006, Bank of America's ratio of equity to total assets was 4.6 percent. At the end of 2020, it was 9.7 percent.

I'm not saying debt is to be avoided. Companies have lots of good reasons to borrow money: to buy equipment, to fund expansion, to finance production, and so on. Interest payments are also tax deductible, resulting in a lower tax bill than an all-equity capital structure. But too much leverage makes the risk of bankruptcy or paralyzing financial

---

11   A good book on GE's problems is Thomas Gryta and Ted Mann's *Lights Out: Pride, Delusion, and the Fall of General Electric* (Boston: Mariner Books, 2020).

distress too high. Outside of the banking industry, be wary of highly levered companies.

As discussed in chapter 7, the amount of debt a firm has can be found on its balance sheet. The amount of interest it pays, its interest expense, is found on its income statement. If most of a firm's operating income is going toward interest, you should be cautious. A small dip in the business could cause the firm to have trouble paying back its lenders.

Diversification

Diversification means owning at least a few different investments. It is a good way to reduce risk. If you own company A, and A goes bankrupt, you lose all your money. If you own A and B, and A goes bankrupt, you only lose half your money. And so on. Diversification is sometimes called investing's only free lunch, since it reduces volatility but does not reduce expected returns.

But diversification cuts both ways. If you have a few really great opportunities, you want to put a lot of money in them. If you have three high-conviction investments, you don't want to mix them with twenty other stocks you don't have an opinion on just to say you're diversified. Putting money in so-so investments just to have more investments is going to weaken your return. If some of your investments have a higher expected return than others, then diversification is no longer a free lunch.

And what happens if some of those twenty stocks we don't have an opinion on drop? Do we sell? Do we buy more? If we understood them, we might conclude they are cheaper and decide to buy more. But since we don't understand them, we might start to think we made a mistake— start to feel uncomfortable. And we might sell.

Some diversification is good, but if you diversify too much you diversify away all your hard work. My advice is five to twenty stock investments is a good number. No matter how exceptional an investment is, there is always the chance that something bad will happen. For instance, for decades Wells Fargo had the reputation of being one of the best-managed banks in the industry. They were a significant holding of Berkshire Hathaway, giving them the unofficial imprimatur of Warren Buffett. Then in 2016 it came to light that they had been creating millions of fraudulent checking and savings accounts. Overnight they went from the top to the bottom of the banking industry, and their stock price suffered.

At the other end, you're only going to have so many high-conviction investments. If you have fifty stocks, are numbers 48 to 50 really going to be as promising as numbers 1 to 3? Probably not. And by including fifty stocks, you've diluted your work away to the point of not being useful. You can always just invest in an index fund if you're more comfortable with that approach.

Extended Risk

Now I'd like to offer an expanded definition of risk that I think will be more useful to the readers of this book. We defined *risk* as "the probability of taking a big loss."

Extended risk is the probability of taking a big loss that then leads to making bad decisions.

Humans are emotional. They fail to anticipate what they will worry about in the future if something bad happens in the present. For instance, say Joe invests a lot of money in Flying Widget at $80 a share, confident that it is worth $100. But now it drops to $50. Joe believes his analysis is correct, but the price drop has created doubt. What's more, the company he works for is having a tough time, and Joe starts to think about the money he'll need to meet expenses if he gets fired. If he sells FWI at $50 he'll have just enough, but it will be tough if it goes down more . . .

You get the picture. A financial loss often leads to other financial worries showing up on the front porch. They may have always been there, but you didn't start to focus on them until you took that loss. The way to avoid a loss leading to a bad decision is to understand your investment process. Know what you're doing. That will give you confidence in your specific investments. Don't let a loss extend from your brokerage account into your head.

But in addition to that, we want a risk control method that works for extended risk. And it's simple.

Keep a Cash Reserve!

This book is written for people who are serious about investing but don't do it full-time. We have jobs and other things in our lives. For us, my advice is to keep a significant cash reserve. Ideally, a year or more of living expenses.

If you have a meaningful cash reserve, you'll be less inclined to get nervous and make a rushed decision if your investments turn against you. If you own Flying Widget International and it starts to crash, you want to decide what to do based on the risk/reward FWI now offers. You don't want to decide what to do because you have a college tuition payment due next week.

Say you do have a $30,000 tuition payment due next week, along with all your other normal bills. If all your spare money is invested in FWI, and FWI plummets, you will start to worry about things getting worse. You might get nervous that you won't have the money for the tuition payment. Your mind conjures images of financial ruin. So instead of deciding what to do with FWI based on *its* current condition, you decide to sell based on *your* current condition. You want to make sure you have the money for the tuition payment, you panic, and you sell at any price.

Many of you are now saying, I won't panic. I'm in control and rational. Maybe. In my experience, it's easy to say that when things are going well. But when things go wrong, the reptilian brain can push the primate brain aside. And even if you stay calm, what happens when your spouse panics and says you need to sell now!

Keeping a year of living expenses is a good place to start. If you're well-off and used to a high standard of living, maybe keep two years. If you have a stable job, such as a tenured teacher or a doctor, then maybe you can get by with six months. But I'd still recommend a year. Even if your income is secure, you could still have a large unanticipated expense.

Your reserve need not be all cash and bank deposits. Some securities are close enough to cash to qualify. For instance, U.S. Treasury bills are basically cash. Bank certificates of deposit (CDs) also qualify (they are insured up to $250,000). If interest rates are very low, then it won't make any difference if you hold cash or a safe security. But if rates are above zero, you may be able to earn some interest on your safety money.

What if your situation is such that you can't come up with half a year or a year's worth of living expenses? Then I'd recommend not investing in stocks and waiting until you do have some cash.

Summary

- Avoiding highly-leveraged companies will help keep risk down.

- Some diversification is good, but buying stocks you don't understand will dilute the value of your good ideas.

- Keep a cash reserve. This will give you the confidence that you can ride out market downturns while still being able to pay your bills.

- Investment losses in the face of impending expenses can lead to bad decisions if you don't have a cash buffer.

Chapter 9:
INVESTING DISCIPLINE

Say you adopt the framework we are developing here. You put together a list of companies you'd consider investing in, you research them, you create a spreadsheet with the relevant financial information, and you invest in stocks with big discounts to their value. Over the first year it goes well and your confidence grows.

But now you find yourself sitting next to Sue at the fifth-grade concert. As the singers file out and the band members file in, she tells you she's done really well in Swiss Francs—up 40 percent. Jeff leans in from a row back and interjects that his financial advisor just recommended he should have 5 percent of his assets in Swiss Francs, on account of adjustments in the world economy. Luckily, the wails of the clarinet drown out your pounding heart.

Pop quiz

You should now a) run home and buy a bunch of Swiss Francs—a currency, you think—or b) stick with the framework you understand and know works. If you've made it this far, then you know at least intellectually you should say a). But for some, knowing isn't enough.

The urge to follow the crowd is bred deep within us. If fifty thousand years ago on the African savanna everyone around you dropped their stone tools and started running, running was probably the right thing to do. But this instinct will not serve you well in investing. It's not that you should do the opposite of the crowd; it's that you should be independent of the crowd. Don't worry about what other people are doing.

In this chapter, we're going to learn some disciplines, some internal nudges, that will keep us on the path to investment success and that will make the path brighter.

Stick to the Plan

A great approach to investing, a great framework, won't be much help if you don't stick to it. This sounds obvious, but you'd be surprised how often people stray because something exciting is happening just over the next hill. I'll just buy a little bitcoin. Or I'll just buy a few copper futures. And then I'll be able tell Sue to stuff it next time she talks about her killing in Swiss Francs.

But wandering into investments you don't understand is not the way to success. You won't know when to get in, when to get out, or what to expect. And the people on the other side of your trades likely are better informed than you.

Don't follow the crowd. You just must accept that there will be times when other people are making money and you aren't. Maybe they're buying into a bubble and will give it back when the bubble bursts. Or maybe they're right and you just missed it. Think of it this way. Say you're a successful surgeon. One day you read mechanical engineers are in demand and getting huge pay raises. Are you going to give up surgery and become a mechanical engineer? Of course not. You've had success being a surgeon and you know you'll have success in the future. And by the time you manage to become a mechanical engineer, the easy money will probably be gone.

Another part of sticking to the plan is correcting mistakes. You will make investing mistakes—we all do. I certainly have. But human nature is such that we don't like to admit mistakes, including to ourselves.

There's an old saying on Wall Street: "Are you long because you like it? Or do you like it because you're long?" Make sure you're in the first camp. Be relentless in correcting mistakes.

Errors come in many forms. The simplest is the typo. Say you typed a bad number into your spreadsheet and ended up buying a company you thought was undervalued but wasn't. Then you catch the error. What should you do? Immediately sell. Don't search around for reasons to justify being long. If you search hard enough, you'll find them. If based on your approach, you never would have bought the stock, correct your mistake, take steps so you won't make that mistake again, and don't give it a second thought.

Now let's take a more subtle error. Say you put a chicken wing company on your list of potentials because you think demand for chicken wings is going to soar. You buy the stock. After some time, you start to wonder about the chicken wing industry. There's more competition than you thought. You start to notice a lot of people eating turkey. You reach the conclusion that the chicken wing industry isn't that great after all. What do you do? Sell. The mistake is a little fuzzier in this example—you misjudged an industry—which makes it easier to do nothing. You could tell yourself you need to think about it more. But if the assessment you have of the industry now would have kept you out, get out now. Other opportunities will come along.

Having an approach with a quantitative model component, as we do, can help. Say your rule is that you won't buy a stock unless it's trading at 60 percent or less of its intrinsic value. One of your stocks is trading at 55 percent of fair value, and you buy it. But now you realize you made a mistake and it's really 80 percent of fair value. Straightforward enough. You broke a clear numeric rule, so you can fix it without agonizing.

There are all sorts of mistakes that can be made, and you'll make lots of them. The bottom line is be relentless on mistakes. Don't try to justify mistaken positions, and don't engage in psychological games. Sell and move on.

Don't Take Any Small Positions

A common behavior is for someone to get to the point where they like a stock but haven't quite done all the work. Maybe they've gotten bored. So they take a small position. "I'll just smart small," they tell themselves. "I'll watch it and see how it goes." If it goes up, they can tell their friends they made money in such and such, even if it wasn't meaningful. If it goes down, well, it's not worth mentioning.

Don't do this! Don't take small positions. Do the work, be confident in your analysis, and take meaningful positions. Note I said, "Be confident in your analysis." I didn't say be certain that you're going to make money. You can never be certain in the stock market. But you know whether you've done the work. If you haven't, do the work or move on to something else.

What's a meaningful position? That's something for you to decide. But I would suggest if you're not willing to put 5 percent of your portfolio into a stock, just wait. Don't buy $100 of something just for the heck of it. You only have so much time for your investments. Why distract yourself with meaningless trades?

Only Trade Once a Year

I admit this one is a tough one, but I recommend only trading once a year. But Adam, you mean I have to stare at the same stocks in my account for, like, months? That's so boring! What about if a great opportunity comes along (and yes, I did all the work)?

Okay, I feel your pain. But hear me out.

If you only rebalance your portfolio once a year, you're forced to evaluate all your current and potential investments at a single point in time. An investment may pop up that looks good, but how do you know another investment isn't better if you're not checking? Maybe you should be adding to an existing position. Or maybe another stock on your list offers a great opportunity, but you just haven't looked in a while.

A Barron's column says ATT is undervalued. You check the numbers and agree ATT is undervalued. But maybe Verizon is a better value. Or some company in a different industry. You could buy ATT and a string of other stocks you evaluate as they come, and at the end of the year find that you could have done better by increasing the size of positions you already have.

We're going to talk more about personal practices later, but what I do is wait for all the fourth-quarter earnings to come out, update my analyses, and then do my trades. This is usually in late February or early March. For the rest of the year, I do little or no trading.

Another advantage of only trading once a year is that it cuts down on trading costs and taxes. Brokerages are increasingly offering commission-free trades. But commission-free does not mean free. You have to pay the bid-ask spread. That is, when you buy, you have to pay a little bit more than the market price, and when you sell, you receive a little bit less than the market price. The algorithmic traders who make billions do so by making markets, not by getting paid commissions.

Also, if you're selling stocks that have gone up, you'll be paying taxes. It's best to defer those. You'll net a lot less on your investments if you pay taxes every year than if you pay your taxes on them once at the end of a long holding period.

The trade-once-a-year rule has exceptions. Say you have a liquidity event. You have to buy a new car you weren't expecting to, or you're starting a business and have to contribute capital. Or you have a big tax bill coming due. Then yes, of course, sell whatever investments you need to. After all, the reason you invest is to have the money to buy things important to you.

What if a really, really good investment comes along? Fine, if you're sure.

William Strunk Jr., in his book *The Elements of Style*, said good writers obey the rules of rhetoric except when they have something to gain by breaking them (paraphrasing). I recommend the same approach. Stick to trading once a year, and deviate from that rule only if you have a good reason.

Hold for the Long Term

Bet you knew this one was coming. Stock investing is a long game. If you buy a stock, you should plan to hold it for years. Here are three reasons: stocks are volatile, investment theses can take a long time to play out, and taxes.

Stocks are volatile. Just because you're right doesn't mean your investment will pay off in two months or even two years. The entire stock market could crash, dragging your stock down with it. But if you're right, the longer you hold, the more likely your investment is to pay off. *The steady accumulation of value will beat out volatility over time.* This reemphasizes the cash reserve argument from last chapter. Position yourself so you can ride out dips. Any money you know you're going to need in the next year, don't put in stocks. Set that money aside. Buy a CD. Even if you've identified a great investment, there's a good chance it will be lower a year from now.

Sometimes you'll hear that your stock should have a catalyst—something that is going to happen that will make the stock go up. If you hold for the long term and your company's earnings increase, you don't need a catalyst. The steady accumulation of value over time will cause the stock price to track upward.

A correct investment thesis can take years to play out. It's much easier to predict what's going to happen than when it's going to happen. Let me say that again: It's much easier to predict what's going to happen than when it's going to happen. A stock staying undervalued for years happens all the time. People's perceptions about a stock can take years to change. Take Microsoft. Microsoft languished for years when it was viewed as a poorly managed, mediocre software maker. (Check out "Steve Ballmer going crazy" on YouTube.) But during this time, Microsoft was building up its Cloud and software-as-service products, all the while maintaining profitability. If you bought Microsoft in 2010, you would have watched it do nothing for a few years. But from the end of 2015 through early 2021, as the market reassessed the company, its stock appreciated about 500 percent.

Taxes offer another reason to hold for the long term. If you sell and buy a lot, you're going to pay a lot more in taxes. Say your capital gains tax rate is 30 percent and you can earn 12 percent on your stock investments. If you sell every year and buy something new, your after-tax annual return will be 8.4 percent (0.7×0.12). If you invest at 12 percent and hold for ten years, your after-tax annual return is 9.5 percent. The difference comes from keeping those tax payments invested and earning. That 1.1 percent a year is going to make a big difference over time.

Summary

1. Stick to the plan. Don't follow the crowd. Stay with the approach you know works.

2. Correct mistakes and move on.

3. Only trade once a year.

4. Don't take any small positions.

5. Hold for the long term.

Chapter 10:
PERSONAL PRACTICES

Congratulations!

You've made it a long way! You've learned what makes a good potential investment, how to value a company, how to manage risk, and how to be disciplined. In this chapter, we're going to pull all these things together and go over the actual steps you'll take. I'll do this by telling what I do. How I've implemented the Straight Up Stock Investing framework over the years.

The approach you take will be personal to you. Maybe your business makes a payout at a certain time during the year, so you want to do your investing right after that. Or maybe you go to a certain conference every year and you want to update your analysis after you get back. Or maybe you want to make your investing decisions after your accountant tells you how much tax you owe. There's a lot of room for personalization in the framework we've developed.

Identify Your Potentials

The first thing you need to do is create a list of potentials. Maybe you already have a list of companies in your head you think might be good. That's great. Start researching them to determine if they have the characteristics of a good potential investment. If you don't have any companies in mind, maybe you have a view on which industries will do well in the future. Find some of the companies in these industries and investigate them. You could read the financial press and start with some of the companies you read about. But the most important thing is to start. Don't get overwhelmed. Just pick a company or two and start.

How do you start? If it's a company that you don't know well, go to its investor relations website and read the front sections of a few of its most recent annual reports: the CEO's letter, the business review, the financial review. The stuff that's in color. After that, I'd watch its year-end webcast. You can listen to an earnings call while driving to work or taking a walk. You won't be able to see the PowerPoints, but I find I learn the most from the analysts' questions. If you're ambitious, you can also read through the most recent 10-K (that's where you'll find the financial data for your spreadsheet).

The companies I follow I've come across in all different ways. Reading the financial press, studying industries, talking to people, figuring out who makes a product I think is great. I read the *Wall Street Journal* cover to cover every day. I definitely recommend reading a lot.

I would go so far as to say that it's hard to be successful in investing if you don't read a lot. People who read have a breadth of knowledge that those who don't usually lack.

But I do want to draw a distinction between reading for information and reading for opinion. When it comes to investing, you want to read for information. Figure out a company's fundamentals—what are its best products, who needs them, what is the outlook for the future? Is the management making good or bad decisions? Research an industry—is it growing or shrinking? What you don't want to do is rely on another person's opinion. If someone you respect says Flying Widget is fantastic, then you may want to put Flying Widget on your list of companies to investigate, but you shouldn't buy Flying Widget just because someone else likes it. If you just follow the opinions of Wall Street analysts or day traders on message boards, you're not going to do well over the long run. Average will be the best you can hope for.

At a higher level, you're reading to establish a structure of understanding for the companies and industries you follow. If you just read Apple's latest earnings release, you know Apple's most recent earnings. If you've read nine years of Apple's earnings releases, when year 10 is released, you're going to have context in which to interpret these earnings. That will make the information much more useful.

Valuation Spreadsheet

Once you have your list of potentials, create a spreadsheet for each one. We saw how to do this in chapter 5. Fill in a few years of historical data. I recommend ten. The history will give you a broader perspective and context in which to understand your company's recent performance. As you identify more companies you'd consider investing in, add them to your spreadsheet.

Next, I update the information in the spreadsheets with year-end results. Fourth-quarter earnings generally come out from early January through late February. (Not all companies have their fiscal year end in December, but most do.) As they do, I'll enter the key numbers into my spreadsheet. My unofficial end of the earnings season is when Berkshire Hathaway reports. Again, usually end of February or the beginning of March.

Figure 10.1.

A Selection of valuations, early 2022

Company	Price	Valuation	IRR
AAPL	167.34	126%	8.1%
CAT	191.95	75%	11.3%
HOG	42.01	100%	10.6%
MSFT	287.65	148%	7.4%
MTB	182.35	60%	13.1%

To make comparison easier, I collect the key information on my companies into its own spreadsheet. I pulled a sample in early 2022, which is displayed in Figure 10.1. (They're just for this discussion, and not to be relied on.) The key indicators are the valuation and the IRR (internal rate of return). Note that Harley-Davidson (HOG) is fairly valued and its IRR is close to 10 percent. In this selection, only M&T Bank is valued at below 60 percent of its intrinsic value[12].

Investing

When all company information is updated, I'll look at all my companies side by side and make my investment decisions. Obviously, the goal is to buy undervalued companies and avoid or sell overvalued companies. The only rule I'm firm on is that I won't buy a stock unless it is valued at 60 percent or less of its fair value. If there is nothing that meets this criterion, I'll just wait. However, in all the years I've been doing this, I've always had at least a couple of stocks flashing green.

You might find this surprising, but I'm perfectly happy holding onto fully valued or moderately overvalued stocks. Remember, if you use a discount rate of 10 percent, then a fairly valued stock should earn 10 percent a year, which is not bad. Even a stock that is moderately overvalued can produce a decent return (check its internal rate of return). Also, if you're holding an overvalued stock, it's probably because it went up. That means you'll pay capital gains taxes if you sell.

Of course, sometimes you'll want to sell a fully valued stock because a great opportunity presents itself. And sometimes a stock will become so overvalued that you feel you need to reduce or sell your position. I don't have a hard rule on this, but often if a stock gets priced at 150 percent of intrinsic value, I'll look to swap it out for another. And if it gets to 200

---

12   M&T Bank has since made a major acquisition, buying People's Bank.

percent I start thinking about selling it outright. My preferred outcome is always to hold.

After my beginning of the year investing, for the rest of the year I do little trading. What I do is pay attention to my potentials. I'll read their earnings announcements. I'll watch their webcasts. I'll tune into their investor days. I'll watch their presentations at banks' investor conferences. I'll read articles written on them. (Read, read, read!) Sometimes I'll look at analyst reports, but as I mentioned, I prefer to do my own research (and you should too).

Some companies I'll track more closely than others. If a company is always overvalued, so there's little chance I'll buy it soon, I may just update the numbers once a year. Of course, it would be better to investigate more carefully, but that may not be the most productive use of your time. Conversely, if there's a company in which I'm considering making a substantial investment, I'll make the effort to get all the information I can about that company.

And then, before you know it, the year is coming to an end and it's time to start up the process again. As you may have noticed, I love investing. I love the investing process. I look forward to updating my model every year and making my investment decisions. It doesn't feel like work to me.

What if you're just getting started with our approach? Maybe your list of potentials so far just has five companies on it, and only one is undervalued. Don't put your whole investment portfolio in that one stock. Remember from chapter 8 that five to twenty stocks is a reasonable number. If your investment portfolio is currently 100 percent invested in an S&P 500 index fund, you could start by moving 20 percent to the undervalued stock. When you have a second undervalued stock, you can move another 20 percent over, and so on.

Deep Dive

I've been doing Shorin-Ryu karate for over twenty-five years. One of the maxims of our style is that it is better to do one kata ten times than to do ten different kata one time each. Why? Because by repeating one kata over and over you'll explore stances, movements, and positions deeper than if you reset each time to a different kata. And this deep exploration will hone skills that will apply to all your kata. Thus, you improve all your kata by immersing yourself in one. The same applies to practicing a musical instrument. Your overall guitar ability will improve by playing one song many times, instead of running through every song you know once.

This concept carries over to investing. By digging deep into one company, you'll come to understand accounting items, industries, corporate strategy—all sorts of things—that you might miss with initial research or when you're just collecting your financial numbers. And this depth of understanding will not only allow you to understand the company you are studying better but it will also help you understand the analogous concepts in other companies. If you take the time to understand how John Deere accounts for, say, the sale and depreciation of leased equipment, you'll be better equipped when you review the statement of cash flows for Caterpillar.

You can read company-specific books. (*Lights Out*, about GE, is a great one.) Many founders write autobiographies that present their path to success. Sam Walton wrote a great one. Did you know some companies have movies about them? There's a movie about the founding of McDonald's (*The Founder*) and a couple about Steve Jobs and Apple. You can search out and read interviews by CEOs. To understand the industry better, you can study the financials of the competitors. You can go to one of its stores and walk around. You get the picture.

You may not have time to go to this depth for every company on your list. But you probably do for one or two. What I suggest is do a deep dive with a company that's been on your radar as a possible purchase. That way, when it comes time to make your investment decision, you'll be that much more prepared. It's also okay to do a deep dive into a company just because you are really interested in it. Years ago, I did very well investing in Marvel Comics. My first exposure to Marvel was not its 10-K.

Here's an achievable goal: Every year, pick at least one company and read its 10-K cover to cover.

Summary

1. Identify your potentials—the companies you'd consider investing in at the right price.

2. Create a valuation spreadsheet for each company on your list.

3. Once a year, evaluate all your potential stock investments side by side and make your investing decisions.

4. Every year, pick one or more of the companies on your list and do a deep dive.

Chapter 11:
THE NUMBER 1 RULE OF INVESTING

Nelson Bunker Hunt and Herbert Hunt were members of the wealthy Texas Hunt oil family.[13] Their family in part inspired the TV show *Dallas*, and at one point Nelson Bunker Hunt was the wealthiest man in America, based on his oil holdings. But the Hunts grew concerned with the future of America and its currency. So in the 1970s, the Hunt family started buying silver. They bought bullion, they bought coins, and they bought silver futures. When they didn't have ready cash, they borrowed and kept on buying. It is believed the Hunts controlled one third of the world's supply of non-government silver.

Their buying pushed the price up. For most of the mid-70s, silver traded for around $5 an ounce. But by the beginning of 1980, it traded for around $40 an ounce, eventually trading for over $50 an ounce on January 18, 1980. People lined up to sell their family silver. Tiffany's—a silver user—took out a full-page ad in the *New York Times* complaining of billionaires driving up the price. Most importantly, the futures exchange changed the rules, making it harder to go long large numbers of futures contracts.

The price of silver began to waiver. Then it began to drop. Then it plummeted. On March 17, 1980, The Hunts' futures account was in deficit, and their broker, Bache, issued a margin call. The problem was that the Hunts didn't have any money to post. You see, they were in debt for over *one billion* dollars, and they had already used that money on previous margin calls.

With the Hunts unable to post margin, Bache began to sell off the Hunts' futures holdings at any price they could get. The price cratered. It came to a head on March 27, 1980, now known to history as Silver

---

13   See Stephen Fay's book *Beyond Greed* (New York: Viking Press, 1982).

Thursday. From a price of $50 two months earlier, silver traded below $11 an ounce. The Hunts had lost billions. Over the next months, they ended up selling most of their remaining holdings. Toward the end of March, Bunker Hunt reflected, "A billion dollars isn't what it used to be."

Thirteen years later, in 1993, the hedge fund Long Term Capital Management began operations.[14] By all accounts it was run by the best of the best. John Meriwether, the CEO, had been the head of Salomon Brothers' Bond Arbitrage Department, one of its most profitable divisions. He brought over much of his team. The firm boasted two Nobel prize winners: Myron Scholes and Robert Merton.

After just four years, the original investors had achieved a return of 185 percent. Many of the partners had borrowed and done even better. Yet just five months later, the Federal Reserve had to orchestrate a takeover of LTCM by a consortium of Wall Street banks. The 185 percent gain had turned into a 77 percent loss.

What happened? Well, you see, what LTCM did was find price discrepancies between similar financial instruments, mostly bonds. The trades were highly likely to make money, but since the spreads were small, they had to take big positions to make a lot of money. And they definitely wanted to make a lot of money. So they borrowed money. A lot of money. Leverage of an unbelievable thirty to one was not uncommon.

Other investors saw how profitable LTCM was, and soon competition from other banks and hedge funds made the spreads tighter, making it tougher to make money. LTCM pushed onward and began to make highly levered trades outside their area of expertise.

But when you're leveraged thirty to one, you don't have much margin for error. It only takes a 3 percent loss to wipe out your equity. In 1998,

---

14   See Roger Lowenstein's book *When Genius Failed* (New York: Random House, 2001).

trades began to move against them. To maintain their capital, they sold off positions. Or at least they tried to. Not only did they find no buyers, but the spreads also got wider and wider, and the losses mounted. The more they tried to sell, the wider the spreads got. LTCM partners suspected the banks whose help they were seeking were actually working against them. This being Wall Street, they were probably right.

The Federal Reserve worried what the effect of an exploding LTCM would have on the markets and took the extraordinary step of organizing a takeover of LTCM by a group of Wall Street banks.

And that was that for Long Term Capital.

But while LTCM was imploding, the U.S. housing market was exploding. In the 1990s and early 2000s, the U.S. housing market boomed. Prices climbed and climbed. Since both bankers and home buyers had only ever seen home prices go up, bankers lent more and more, and buyers borrowed more and more. Not only did the government just watch this, but it also pitched in by encouraging banks to lend to people who had low incomes and were therefore at higher risk of not being able to make loan payments. Banks were highly leveraged. Homeowners were highly leveraged. Investors were highly leveraged. Everyone was highly leveraged.

You know what happened next. In 2008, the bottom fell out. Over the period from July 2006 through February 2012, the price of houses dropped 27 percent. As the economy weakened, borrowers had trouble making their mortgage payments and were forced to sell their homes or simply toss the bank the keys if the mortgage was more than the value of the house. Banks sold houses as fast as they could. At the same time, they were calling in loans, forcing prices down even more. Builders seeing what was happening tried to sell their current projects at any price. Collapse across the economy ensued. A sad period in our country's financial history.

What do these three events have in common? In all cases someone owned something and had to sell it. They were forced sellers. The Hunts had to sell silver, LTCM had to sell sophisticated financial positions, and homeowners and banks had to sell houses. In all cases, it was a disaster for the seller.

Here is the number 1 rule of investing: *Never be a forced seller.*

Never be a forced seller!

Being a forced seller is the financial equivalent of jumping into a woodchipper.

There are even more recent incidents I could mention. For instance, in 2021 the hedge fund Archegos borrowed too much money and was forced sell its stocks at any price to pay back loans. Not only did they go out of business, but one of their lenders, Credit Suisse, took a multi-billion-dollar loss, with many people losing their jobs. Note that Archegos blew up owning stocks during a tremendous bull market. When you are highly leveraged, not much has to go wrong.

When you must sell, you are unlikely to get a good price. And if other people are in the same boat as you or potential buyers know you must sell, the price of whatever you're selling could crash. After all, if you know the Hunts are being forced to sell silver, are you going to step up and buy one tick down? No. You'll either put in a low bid or just wait and see how low the price goes. It's the Hunts in a rush, not you.

The housing crisis of 2008 was made worse because so many people were in the same boat. Homeowners, builders, and banks all had to sell at once. There were buyers coming into the market, but not enough to absorb all the supply. So prices collapsed.

A common thread in our examples is debt. The Hunts borrowed, LTCM borrowed, homeowners took mortgages, Archegos borrowed. Debt makes the upside higher. But it also makes the downside lower. And it's not symmetric. If you borrowed to buy Flying Widget and it goes up, you don't have to buy more. But if you borrowed and it goes down, you may have to sell to pay off your loans, and that could push the price down further.

My advice is to avoid leverage, or at least avoid more than you can handle if things go against you.

Also, big losses are scary. They cloud your decision-making process and put your mind in a dark place. Big losses caused by leverage may compel you to sell to end your anxiety and worry.

Remember extended risk. The risk of an investment isn't just that it might produce a loss. The risk is that it might produce a loss and that loss will lead to a bad decision.

Another cause of forced selling is investing money you'll need soon. Say you have $15,000. And say you've promised to take your family on a summer vacation to Italy that will cost $10,000. You do a perfect analysis and determine that Flying Widget is trading for 60 percent of its fair value. So, you invest $15,000 in March and plan to sell $10,000 worth in June to pay for the vacation. But now the price drops. In April, your position is worth only $10,000, exactly what you'll need for the vacation you've promised your family. You check your analysis, and you're confident you did everything right. The stock is now even more undervalued. But if it goes down any more, you won't be able to pay for the vacation. You sell, and lock in your vacation.

It is better to be underinvested in a position you can hold onto than to be overinvested in a position you'll have to sell if it goes against you.

Now, forced selling isn't all bad. Sometimes someone else is the forced seller and you can take advantage of it. Not perhaps the most compassionate angle on investing, but if someone needs a buyer and you step up, you're helping them out. So, if you read about a hedge fund blowing up, you may want to check if any of its stockholdings is on your potential list.

If a stock on your list is in a forced sale, be patient. Don't rush in and buy while it is dropping. You may think something can't possibly go lower, only to find that it does. During the dumping process, fundamental valuations won't matter. Other potential buyers probably don't have ready valuations and will take some time to complete them. Assume you have a buying window of a couple weeks, and recheck your analysis. House prices peaked in 2006 and didn't reach their bottom until 2012.

You may think you'll never be forced to sell. You're probably right. But take the steps to make sure.

Summary

- The Number 1 Rule of Investing is *never be a forced seller*.

CONCLUSION

My high school English teacher said the key to teaching is to follow three steps: tell'em what you're gonna tell'em, tell'em, then tell'em what you told'em. We're now at the part of the book where I tell you what I told you.

Identification, valuation, and personalization. These are the three pieces of the Straight Up Stock Investing method. They will take you far.

Identification

You can't be an expert, or even reasonably informed, on every company. But you can be well informed on a lot of companies. How many? That will depend on how much work you're willing to put in. Maybe it's fifteen. Maybe it's one hundred. But whatever the number, you need to narrow the universe of stocks in which you might invest to that number. Those are the companies you understand. That is your gold mine. When the opportunity comes to buy shares in one of those companies, you'll take a big position with confidence and won't be shaken by bounces in price.

Limiting yourself to a vetted list of companies also imposes a valuable discipline. You won't make an impulse purchase of a stock that someone is touting. If someone is hyping a company that's on your list, you'll already possess a base of knowledge, and a decision to invest or not will be guided by the foundation you've prepared. If a company isn't on your list, you don't buy it. You might want to research that firm and consider adding it to your list of potentials. But it must go on your list first.

What firms go on your list of potentials? Firms whose businesses and industries are likely to prosper in the future. These firms have an earnings tailwind, which will provide ongoing support to the stock price. Don't worry about the price of the stock at this stage. You're listing companies that are winners. You'll consider the price as part of your decision to invest or not.

What firms stay off your list? Firms whose businesses and industries are likely to deteriorate. Can't you make money buying undervalued companies in a declining industry? Maybe. But you're always trading, paying taxes, and having to look for the next investment. In rising businesses, time is your friend. In waning businesses, time is your enemy.

What are some of the characteristics of good firms? Here are a few: good prospects for the industry, strong earnings growth, a valuable intangible, a strong CEO, pricing power, network effect, high customer switching costs, and being the low-cost producer.

What are some characteristics to avoid? Here are a few of those: commodity business, lots of competition, strong unions, lots of capex needed, and the opposite of what's in the good list.

And don't forget what you bring to the table. Your skills, interests, education, and professional experiences. All of these will help you decide which companies and industries to set your sights on. Your experience will also provide a substructure upon which to build your foundation of understanding. Whether you know it or not, you have advantages in the investing world. Use them.

Valuation

Once you have your list of stocks, your goal is to buy some of them at prices well below the value of their future cash flow streams. This value is computed by discounting your estimate of future cash flows back to the present. How cheap a stock must be before investing is up to you. I use 60 percent. That is, I target buying stocks on my list that are priced at 60 percent or less of their intrinsic value.

You're going to make a lot of estimates, so you'll never be precisely correct. And you'll make mistakes. But over the long term, you'll have more investment success making informed decisions based on a solid framework than you will investing based on the opinions of others.

The analytics are straightforward for companies that are established and growing at normal rates: Forecast future cash flows based on 1) recent cash flows and 2) estimated growth rates and discount back to the present. It's also helpful to compute the internal rate of return. The IRR doesn't give you any new information, but it presents the result as an interest rate, a construct for which most investors have an intuition. There is no reason to sell fairly valued companies. Remember, if you use a 10 percent discount rate, then a fairly valued company will yield 10 percent a year.

For high-growth companies and companies that are losing money while they build, the framework is the same. With these companies, however, forecasting future earnings is tougher. Extrapolating recent earnings usually doesn't work. You'll need to directly estimate future cash flows without recourse to past performance. Sometimes the company itself or Wall Street analysts can be helpful.

Personalization

You have your list of stocks. You know what they're worth. But there are still some things you must do. You must manage risk, you must know how much to buy, you must know when to buy.

There are two ways to think about risk. The first is to acknowledge there is some chance you'll take a big loss and to take that into consideration. When that big loss occurs, it's just one more day at the investing office. You start the next day facing the same distribution of outcomes. The second is to acknowledge there is some chance you'll take a big loss and to also acknowledge that a big loss is going to affect your investment decision-making. If you're Mr. Spock, the first definition is all you need. But the rest of us should consider the second definition.

A financial loss can get you thinking about the next financial loss, which can get you thinking about all the things you won't be able to do, which can cause you to bail on an investment. You want to avoid this. You want to make investment decisions based on the circumstances of your potential investments, not on the circumstances of you.

Too much debt can be the catalyst for a big financial loss. I'd guess that too much leverage is the cause of most personal financial blowups and most economy-wide financial crises (such as 2008). If you borrow money, make sure you're able to cover it should you have a less than perfect financial outcome.

The risk management tool I recommend is to hold a cash reserve. How big? A year's worth of living expenses is not a bad target. If your income is secure, or you have a big bonus coming, maybe a little less. But whatever you choose, a cash buffer is your primary risk control tool. Your buffer does not have to be literally cash. Short-term treasuries and CDs are close to risk free and could earn you some interest.

Pick a time during the year to evaluate all your investment opportunities and make your trades. Someone will tell you about an exciting new company, and you'll be tempted to take out your wallet. Not so fast! Instead, funnel that adrenaline into learning about this exciting new company. Then, when your time for investing comes, you can evaluate that company in the context of all your other opportunities.

When you make an investment, go big! You probably have a handful of good ideas. You need to put them to work for you. But if you only invest $100, you're not buying an investment, you're buying a distraction. Taking small positions is the most salient symptom of the investing laziness disease. People buy small amounts so they can tell themselves they're taking action when really they're covering for not completing their research. Never tell yourself that you'll just start with a small position and see how it goes.

Hold for the long term. In this case, the standard investing advice is correct. If you trade a lot, you're going to pay lots of taxes, incur lots of transactions costs, and will always be searching for new places to put your money. It's fine to hold a stock that's fairly valued or a little overvalued. If you've used a ten percent discount rate, then a fairly valued stock will yield ten percent a year. Nothing wrong with that. An investment that yields ten percent a year will double in value every seven years.

Finally, here is the one rule you must never forget: Never be a forced seller! If you're forced to sell your investments at any price, years of hard work can be washed away in moments. You'll want to bend over and puke. Think ahead and avoid putting yourself in a position where you might have to sell at any price. Know your future expenses, and don't use more debt than you can handle.

Warren Buffett famously said that he attempts to be fearful when others are greedy and to be greedy only when others are fearful.

I respectfully offer a slight rephrasing. You should be fearful when others are greedy and be *prepared* when others are fearful. I hope this book has helped prepare you for investing success.

ACKNOWLEDGEMENTS

I thank Jess Gaspar and Maddy Kozower for reading an earlier draft. This book has benefitted from their suggestions and corrections.

AUTHOR BIO

Adam Dunsby co-founded three successful investment companies, served as a Representative in the Connecticut legislature, and as the first selectman of Easton, Connecticut. He holds a BS and PhD in finance from the Wharton School of the University of Pennsylvania.

Adam has taught finance at Sacred Heart and Fairfield Universities. He is a co-author of Commodity Investing and a partner at Mansby Capital.